You Can Do Hard Things

DEVOTIONAL

You Can Do Hard Things

DEVOTIONAL

SHERILYNN ALCALA

Copyright © 2021 by SheriLynn Alcala.

All rights reserved. No part of this publication may be reproduced, distributed, or transmitted in any form or by any means, including photocopying, recording, or other electronic or mechanical methods, without the prior written permission of the publisher, except in the case of brief quotations embodied in critical reviews and certain other noncommercial uses permitted by copyright law. For permission requests, write to the publisher at the address below.

Fedd Books

P.O. Box 341973

Austin, TX 78734

www.thefeddagency.com

Published in association with The Fedd Agency, Inc., a literary agency.

Unless otherwise noted, all Scripture quotations are taken from THE HOLY BIBLE, NEW INTERNATIONAL VERSION®, NIV® Copyright © 1973, 1978, 1984, 2011 by Biblica, Inc.® Used by permission. All rights reserved worldwide.

Scripture quotations marked (NLT) are taken from the Holy Bible, New Living Translation, copyright ©1996, 2004, 2015 by Tyndale House Foundation. Used by permission of Tyndale House Publishers, Inc., Carol Stream, Illinois 60188. All rights reserved.

Scripture quotations taken from the (NASB®) New American Standard Bible®, Copyright © 1960, 1971, 1977, 1995, 2020 by The Lockman Foundation. Used by permission. All rights reserved. www.lockman.org.

Scripture quotations marked (KJV) are taken from the King James Version of the Bible.

Scripture quotations marked (ESV) are taken from the ESV® Bible (The Holy Bible, English Standard Version®), copyright © 2001 by Crossway, a publishing ministry of Good News Publishers. Used by permission. All rights reserved.

Scripture quotations marked (NKJV) are taken from the New King James Version®. Copyright © 1982 by Thomas Nelson. Used by permission. All rights reserved.

Scripture quotations marked CSB have been taken from the Christian Standard Bible®, Copyright © 2017 by Holman Bible Publishers. Used by permission. Christian Standard Bible® and CSB® are federally registered trademarks of Holman Bible Publishers.

Scripture quotations marked (GNT) are from the Good News Translation in Today's English Version, Second Edition. Copyright © 1992 by American Bible Society. Used by permission.

Scripture quotations marked (MSG) are taken from THE MESSAGE, copyright © 1993, 1994, 1995, 1996, 2000, 2001, 2002 by Eugene H. Peterson. Used by permission of NavPress. All rights reserved. Represented by Tyndale House Publishers, Inc.

Scripture quotations marked (NCV) are taken from the New Century Version®. Copyright © 2005 by Thomas Nelson. Used by permission. All rights reserved.

Scripture quotations marked (TPT) are from The Passion Translation®. Copyright © 2017, 2018 by Passion & Fire Ministries, Inc. Used by permission. All rights reserved. ThePassionTranslation.com.

Scripture quotations marked (BSB) are taken from The Holy Bible, Berean Study Bible, BSB. Copyright ©2016, 2020 by Bible Hub. Used by Permission. All Rights Reserved Worldwide.

Scripture quotations marked (CEV) are taken from the Contemporary English Version Copyright © 1991, 1992, 1995 by American Bible Society, Used by Permission.

Cover Design: Deryn Pieterse

ISBN: 978-1-949784-81-7

eISBN: 978-1-949784-82-4

Library of Congress Control Number: 2021918072

Printed in the United States of America

First Edition 22 23 24 25 26 / 9 8 7 6 5 4 3 2 1

I want to dedicate this to all the women out there in that baby-raising season of life; the ones putting in the blood, sweat, and tears to build their businesses; the ones just trying to make it through each day; and the ones who have those burning dreams in their hearts that they long to pursue. I see you, I feel you, I've been there, and I am there. When you grow tired, when you feel weary, when you don't know if you have anything else to give—I pray that something from one of these pages speaks to your heart. Never forget that your heavenly Father has for you exceedingly, abundantly more than you could ever ask or imagine. You were created for such a time as this.

I came so that they would have life, and have it abundantly.

JOHN 10:10 NASB

CONTENTS

INTRODUCTION: START DREAMING 13
DAY 1: FIRST THINGS FIRST 16
DAY 2: REFRAME YOUR TO-DO LIST 18
DAY 3: STINKING THINKING 20
DAY 4: WHAT SITS ON YOUR THRONE? 22
DAY 5: MINDSET OF ABUNDANCE 24
DAY 6: IMMEASURABLY MORE 26
DAY 7: AN AUDIENCE OF ONE 28
DAY 8: KNOW YOUR WORTH 30
DAY 9: GRUMBLING OR GRATITUDE 32
DAY 10: RUNNING ON EMPTY 34
DAY 11: REJECTION 36
DAY 12: ANCHORED 38
DAY 13: WHERE IS YOUR FOCUS? 40
DAY 14: THE COMPARISON TRAP 42
DAY 15: PROTECT YOUR THOUGHTS 44
DAY 16: PEOPLE DON'T BELONG ON PEDESTALS 46
DAY 17: STRENGTHS AND WEAKNESSES 48
DAY 18: NO SUCH THING AS AN ORDINARY MASTERPIECE ... 50
DAY 19: LIVING FOR ETERNITY 52
DAY 20: LET GO OF THE WHEEL, SIS 54
DAY 21: FAIL FORWARD 56
DAY 22: RIGHT NOW 58
DAY 23: FRIENDSHIP 60
DAY 24: MUSTARD SEEDS 62
DAY 25: OUT WITH THE OLD, IN WITH THE NEW 64
DAY 26: FORGIVENESS 66
DAY 27: FEELING ALONE 68
DAY 28: THE GREAT DEFENDER 70
DAY 29: POURING FROM AN EMPTY CUP 72
DAY 30: YOU'RE NOT FORGOTTEN 74

DAY 31: A PROMISE DELAYED	76
DAY 32: INNER CIRCLE	78
DAY 33: PRAY CONTINUALLY	80
DAY 34: ASKING OUR FATHER	82
DAY 35: FROM BITTER TO BLESSED	84
DAY 36: DREAMER & DOER	86
DAY 37: PEOPLE PLEASING	88
DAY 38: ALTOGETHER LOVABLE	90
DAY 39: NAGGING THOUGHTS	92
DAY 40: REPLACING JEALOUSY WITH JOY	94
DAY 41: RESTLESS WORLD	96
DAY 42: TAKING THOUGHTS CAPTIVE	98
DAY 43: HAIR COUNT	100
DAY 44: HOLD MY BAGGAGE	102
DAY 45: CHOOSING KINDNESS	104
DAY 46: TRUST	106
DAY 47: KNOW WHOSE YOU ARE	108
DAY 48: TRUE HAPPINESS	110
DAY 49: PUT THE MEASURING TAPE AWAY	112
DAY 50: THE BEST PATHWAY	114
DAY 51: OVERCOMING FAILURE	116
DAY 52: VISION	118
DAY 53: THE THING ABOUT SETBACKS	120
DAY 54: EQUIPPED FOR WHAT-IFS	122
DAY 55: TRADING TRAGEDY FOR TESTIMONY	124
DAY 56: SEASONS	126
DAY 57: TREASURE AND PONDER	128
DAY 58: DON'T RUSH; BE STILL	130
DAY 59: COMFORT ZONE	132
DAY 60: WHAT'S IN YOUR HAND?	134
ENDNOTES	139

Introduction

START DREAMING

A lot can happen in sixty days.

It's enough time to grow summer squash.
It's enough time to take a college summer course.
It's enough time to lose a guy six times.
And it's enough time to change your life.

That's what I pray these next sixty days will do for you, not because of anything I've written, but because of God's truths embedded throughout these pages. He has big plans and wants to do amazing things through you. It'll be hard work, but the good news is, you can do hard things! Have I mentioned that yet?

I strongly believe God has put unique dreams on our hearts, and when we walk with Him as we pursue those dreams, we become unstoppable. He has given us an abundant life, and He is waiting for us to discover it in all its fullness.

I want you to decide to carve out just a few minutes to read these daily devotions and pray. I know, I know: your days are already jam-packed, and your to-do list only seems to grow and never diminish. But in this fast-paced world, where your Chick-fil-A is hot and ready before you even reach the end of the drive-thru line, I want you to slow down, pause, and make time for the One who truly matters.

These devotions are basically bite-size lessons I've learned—most of them the hard way. Nevertheless, I've learned them by leaning into God's unchanging Word. I tried to pick topics I deal with daily: worry, fear, comparison, and not being enough. I wanted to make you aware of the lies we often listen to and replace them with God's truth! His words, truths, and promises are the same yesterday, today, and tomorrow!

In case you haven't learned this lesson yet, let me tell you from my own experience that we can't walk through this crazy life alone. When we try, it's not a pretty sight. We have to stay close to our source of strength and let Him pour into us, lead us, and fill us up! When I operate out of my own strength, I fail every time, but when I surrender to God and let Him carry me, we win.

Will you commit over the next sixty days to spend some time with the Lord (and me) each day? Maybe you have never done a devotional. Good. Let's do this together. Put your phone on silent or airplane mode, set aside your to-do list and distractions, and focus on Jesus. Time spent with the Lord is never wasted. I can't wait to hear what He speaks to you, shows you, and sets you free from. Let's do it, sis!

—**SheriLynn**

Day 1

FIRST THINGS FIRST

But seek ye first the kingdom of God, and his righteousness, and all these things shall be added unto you. MATTHEW 6:33 KJV

Do you ever feel like there's just not enough time? Like if you had thirty hours in the day, then maybe you could do it all?

I often feel like my to-do list multiplies as the day goes on. Between chauffeuring my kids to their endless activities, working, and keeping up with the house, I end the day feeling both drained and like I haven't done enough. This morning, I woke up, poured a cup of coffee, and started a load of laundry, while simultaneously packing lunches for my kids. How am I supposed to do it all? How do I fit it all in? Why do I feel like my to-do list just won't end? Wait, maybe that's the problem: I'm trying to squeeze it all in and do it all by myself. Where does my heavenly Father fit in? Where is His time?

I don't know about you, but when my calendar fills up, spending time with God gets pushed to the bottom of the to-do list. I make excuses and say I just don't have time; there are other things I need to do. But Matthew 6 tells us that our heavenly Father knows our needs and that when we seek Him first, our needs will be met. Daily time with Him is crucial; His presence fills us with the hope, peace, and strength we need to take on whatever comes our way. Sit and talk with Him; invite Him to walk with you throughout the day and experience the peace that only His presence provides.

PRAYER: Lord, I need You. My days feel out of control when I don't spend them walking with You. Forgive me for not making time for You. In the morning when I rise, give me Jesus, even before that cup of coffee—only then will I experience peace and joy and be able to gracefully handle it all.

DO THE HARD THING: Commit to carving out time first thing every morning to spend with God, whether it is ten minutes or sixty minutes. Time with Him is never lost.

Day 2

REFRAME YOUR TO-DO LIST

I will give thanks to the Lord because of his righteousness; I will sing the praises of the name of the Lord Most High.
PSALM 7:17

We all have items on our to-do list that we dread. And if you don't, you're either a liar or a saint. If the former, keep reading; if the latter, you can probably just return this book. When we fixate on the things we dread, our minds and hearts become filled with complaints and negativity: "Why, why, why? Why do I have to go to that parent-teacher meeting this morning—would an email not suffice? Why do I have to take my car to the dealership to have the breaks fixed again; I'll lose a good two hours of my day! And then two back-to-back work calls this evening? No, thank you."

It helps me to reframe the things I'm not looking forward to through the lens of gratitude. What if we replaced the words "have to" with the words "get to"? And not just that, but what if we sincerely looked for the good and purpose in each activity? I get to meet with my precious daughter's teacher, who is sowing into my child every single day. I get to take my car to the dealership to have the breaks fixed; it was only ten years ago that we had a car that needed to have the brakes replaced but we couldn't afford to get them fixed. I'm thankful that we can afford to have a safer vehicle. I get to hop on two work calls for a job that I actually love. In a time when we faced a pandemic and people lost jobs, my job has thrived and my team grew, and what an enormous blessing that was.

The tasks will stay the same but the lens through which we choose to look at them will make all the difference in the world. Choosing to live with gratitude means no longer treating our blessings like curses. When we change our perspective, we begin to see the blessings everywhere.

PRAYER: Thank You, Jesus, that I get to live this beautiful life. Thank You for all the blessings You've provided for me and my family. Please help me see my day through the lens of gratitude. Help me see the blessings You've laid before me today.

DO THE HARD THING: I challenge you to write out your to-do list for the day but use the phrase "I get to" before each task.

Day 3

STINKING THINKING

Therefore, put on every piece of God's armor so you will be able to resist the enemy in the time of evil. Then after the battle you will still be standing firm. **EPHESIANS 6:13 NLT**

Have you ever had a dream or a goal that you talk yourself out of within minutes of discovering it? You convince yourself that you're setting yourself up for failure or being unrealistic or impractical. You have thoughts like, *I don't want to be let down or disappointed, so isn't it better to stay safe?* Or, *I'm pretty sure I missed my chance to do anything great in this world anyway. There are so many other people out there who are already doing what I once dreamed of doing. Plus, I probably wouldn't have been any good at it anyway.* Lies—all those thoughts are lies of the Enemy!

John 10:10 tells us exactly what our Enemy sets out to do: steal, kill, and destroy. There is a real devil who wants to steal those God-given dreams. Ephesians 6:12 warns us that, "our struggle is not against flesh and blood, but against the rulers, against the authorities, against the powers of this world's darkness, and against the spiritual forces of evil in the heavenly realms" (BSB). There is a war we must fight daily. When those thoughts come—and they will, sis—it is up to us to take those lies captive immediately and replace them with the truth according to the Word of God!

Next time you think, *I can't accomplish that,* replace it with this truth: God will "equip you with everything good for doing his will" (Hebrews 13:21).

Next time you think, *I'm not enough,* replace it with this: "For we are God's masterpiece. He has created us anew in Christ Jesus, so we can do the good things he planned for us long ago" (Ephesians 2:10 NLT).

Every time you go down that road of stinking thinking, stop yourself. Don't let the Enemy steal your dreams, peace, or joy. Exchange those negative thoughts for positive ones because you're a daughter of the King.

PRAYER: Lord, please help me fight the lies of the Enemy. I pray that Your words saturate my heart and mind so that when a lie comes, I can fight it with truth. Thank You for equipping me with everything I need and always being present with me.

DO THE HARD THING: Every time you catch yourself in stinking thinking, I want you to stop yourself and replace the negative thought with the truth. Let's take it a step further, though: I want you to speak the counter thought out loud.

Day 4

WHAT SITS ON YOUR THRONE?

Jesus replied: "'Love the Lord your God with all your heart and with all your soul and with all your mind.' This is the first and greatest commandment." **MATTHEW 22:37-38**

Sometimes our schedules, hearts, minds, and priorities get so out of whack that we begin worshiping parts of our lives other than God. We don't intentionally do it; most of the time it happens gradually, which is why it's important to check in and ask yourself, "Who or what is sitting on the throne of my life?"

There have been unhealthy seasons when my job has sat on the throne; it got all of me, and everyone and everything else was pushed to the side. There have been times—more than I want to admit—when my children sat on the throne. I put them above my husband and time with the Lord; everything revolved around them. For you it could be a promotion, money, your spouse, your appearance, social media, and so on. What are you putting first? Who or what consumes your mind and thoughts all day long?

When something or someone other than God sits on the throne of our lives, we won't be able to live abundantly. God wants to be the one sitting on the throne of your life. He wants more than two hours on Sundays, thirty seconds before each meal, or only when you need something. He wants to walk with you throughout your entire day and night. Are you just fitting God in when you can, or is He at the top of the list and on the throne of your life?

PRAYER: God, I confess that I've placed other things on the throne of my life, but I know that is Your rightful place. Help me to love You with all my heart, soul, and mind. Help me live in the abundance You offer through Your presence.

DO THE HARD THING: Who or what are you putting first in your life? Write out your priorities, starting with the most important, and then see if you need to do a little rearranging.

Day 5

MINDSET OF ABUNDANCE

Rejoice with those who rejoice. ROMANS 12:15

Do you ever feel like you're one (or ten) steps behind other people? Like they're out there running circles around you while you're just trying to catch your breath? Do you ever see other people accomplishing your dreams and then you let go of that dream because it's already been done and you're sure they did it better than you ever could? Yeah, me either.

Sometimes I feel like there isn't enough to go around. I dreamed of writing a book for years—and then someone else went out and wrote a book with so many of my ideas! It's like she read my mind or something. And I thought, *I guess I missed my chance.* I wanted to start a fashion blog and then one of my girlfriends started one. And I thought, *I'm sure our friends will read hers, so never mind that.* I have been working so hard for a promotion in my company and out of nowhere comes this new girl with less experience, and she just passed me up! To make things worse, the whole company loves her. What am I? Chopped liver? I feel invisible. My best friend and I have always been in similar seasons in life until now. Their family business took off—like really took off—so they're financially set for life. But I'm still over here clipping coupons. When will my family catch a break?

Have you ever had those thoughts? I have, more times than

I want to admit. As I was moping one day about missing my chance on this or that, the Holy Spirit spoke to me in a whisper and reminded me to "rejoice with those who rejoice." Umm, wait, you mean I have to be happy for them because they're living their best life while I'm over here wishing for mine? Yes! Your girlfriend over there achieving her dream isn't taking anything away from you. She did not steal a piece of your pie. Don't let envy or jealousy creep in. Don't you dare throw in the towel and give up on your dreams because someone else is accomplishing theirs. Let those who win around you inspire you and show you that you can win, too. Let go of that scarcity mindset, and instead embrace a mindset of abundance. We're all children of the Most High King. There is more than enough to go around, my friend.

PRAYER: Lord, please help me surrender my scarcity mindset and adopt the mindset of abundance. Please give me courage as I follow my dreams and help me rejoice as others accomplish their dreams too. Thank You for Your abundant love and Your everlasting promises. Amen.

DO THE HARD THING: List some of your dreams on your heart as if they have already happened. For example, "I wrote my first book" or "I have a lifestyle blog." Decide right now to live with an abundance mindset because there is enough for us all.

Day 6

IMMEASURABLY MORE

Now to him who is able to do immeasurably more than all we ask or imagine, according to his power that is at work within us, to him be glory in the church and in Christ Jesus throughout all generations, for ever and ever! Amen. EPHESIANS 3:20-21

I have all these dreams in my heart, but they seem impossible. I want to do great things in my life and for the kingdom of God, but every time I start to pursue them, doubt, insecurity, and fear creep in. What if I try and fail?

Have you ever felt like that? Almost every time a new dream is birthed in my heart, I start to doubt it: Can I really do it? Do I have what it takes? Am I strong enough? The answer is no. I, alone, can't do it. But guess what? I don't have to tackle those dreams alone. I'm not in this race by myself, and neither are you. The Author of those dreams, the One who birthed them inside of you, is right there with you. The word of God says, "'Not by might nor by power, but by my Spirit' says the Lord Almighty" (Zechariah 4:6). If we had what it took to accomplish our dreams by ourselves, I think our prideful human nature wouldn't recognize our need to rely on God.

So, realizing and acknowledging that you and I are not enough is a good thing! We need our heavenly Father's help, and He is more than willing and able to give it. Today, find comfort in knowing you can accomplish your dreams when you're plugged into the Source of the dreams, the Dream Giver. And He can do immeasurably more than we could ask or imagine.

PRAYER: Today, I bring all my dreams before You. I know I can't achieve these alone. I know I need You with me. Help me believe You can do immeasurably more with my dreams than I could ask or imagine.

DO THE HARD THING: List five dreams you have. I don't care if they're big or small. Then I want you to surrender those dreams to the Lord. Stop trying to carry and accomplish them alone. Take a few minutes and pray that God would not only give you the strength to accomplish them but that He also would do immeasurably more with them.

Day 7

AN AUDIENCE OF ONE

Am I now trying to win the approval of human beings, or of God? Or am I trying to please people? If I were still trying to please people, I would not be a servant of Christ.
GALATIANS 1:10

It feels good to hear praises, compliments, and applause from others. It feels good when you get the approval you have been striving for or the pat on the back you so badly wanted. But I have learned this past year that I can't live my life or pursue my dreams based on the praises I do or don't receive.

I have always been pretty good at ignoring the haters. I dedicated a whole chapter in my last book, *You Can Do Hard Things*, to tuning out critics. But as important as it is to not let criticism distract you or stop you, it is equally important not to live for the acclamations. For much of my adult life, I worked extra hard in hopes of being noticed. That was fine and dandy when I received the recognition, but what about when I didn't? What about when someone I was trying to gain approval from didn't notice? I would even say that feeling forgotten by those you admire is infinitely more painful than being criticized by a stranger on social media.

As I walked through a season where I felt forgotten, ignored, and unnoticed, the Lord gently reminded me that my job is to live for an audience of one, Jesus Christ. His approval and validation are all I need. He is the only heart I need to worry about pleasing. Wow, how freeing it is to live in that way. It takes the heavy burdens of what others may think—good or bad—off my shoulders. When we learn to walk in the acceptance we already have through Christ, we'll have everything we need when we face rejection or even those feelings of being forgotten.

Just as we have to tune out the critics, we must also learn to tune out our desire for praise from others.

PRAYER: Help me live for an audience of one. When my attention is divided and I look for the approval of others, I lose focus on You and Your promises. People are fickle, but You're unchanging. Help me keep my eyes on You.

DO THE HARD THING: What are the areas in your life where you have tried to gain the approval of people instead of the Lord? Write out any examples you can think of and decide today to surrender those areas to the Lord.

Day 8

KNOW YOUR WORTH

But you are a chosen people, a royal priesthood, a holy nation, God's special possession, that you may declare the praises of him who called you out of darkness into his wonderful light.
1 PETER 2:9

One morning, I prayed, "Who am I that You would want to use me, Lord? The mistakes seem to pile up; I try and then I fail. I feel like a fraud at times. I do not feel worthy to even be a child of God, let alone carry out Your work." As I was praying, His gentle Spirit replied with, "Who am I that I wouldn't want to use you?"

Does anyone else battle with those feelings of unworthiness? When you dive into the Bible, you can find story after story of great men and women who battled with their own feelings of unworthiness. In Exodus 4, Moses argued with the Lord about not going to Pharaoh on the Israelites' behalf because he didn't feel qualified: "But Moses pleaded with the LORD, 'O Lord, I'm not very good with words. I never have been, and I'm not now, even though you have spoken to me. I get tongue-tied, and my words get tangled'" (v. 10). God was not having it. "Then the LORD asked Moses, 'Who makes a person's mouth? Who decides whether people speak or do not speak, hear or do not hear, see or do not see? Is it not I, the LORD? Now go! I will be with you as you speak, and I will instruct you in what to say'" (vv. 11-12

NLT). Although Moses doubted himself, the Lord reminded him who his heavenly Father and Creator was!

Romans 3:23 tells us that we've all sinned and fallen short of God's glory. And Titus 3:5 reminds us that "he saved us, not because of the righteous things we had done, but because of his mercy. He saved us through the washing of rebirth and renewal by the Holy Spirit." Do I deserve the mercy and grace He gives me time and time again? No, but I'm given it freely and so are you. We'll never be enough on our own, but with God beside us, working in us and through us, we're more than enough. You, my friend, are worthy in His eyes.

PRAYER: God, some days I do not feel worthy, but I'm worthy because I'm Your child and because of the grace and mercy You freely extend to me. Help me see my worthiness through Your eyes.

DO THE HARD THING: What are some things you feel the Lord has called you or instructed you to do but you have been arguing with Him like Moses? Is He telling you to start a Bible study, lead a small group, or take that first step toward a blog or podcast? List some things that come to your heart and then ask God if now is the right time to start.

_____

_____

_____

_____

Day 9

GRUMBLING OR GRATITUDE

I will praise you, LORD, with all my heart; I will tell of all the marvelous things you have done. PSALM 9:1 NLT

Have you ever been asked what your high and low of the week was? Then you spend five minutes talking about your lows, but when it comes to your high, you draw a blank? It's often easier for me to see what is going wrong in a situation than what is going right. It is easier for me to look at my flaws than my gifts, and I often catch myself complaining more than giving thanks.

I'm not a psychologist, but this tendency to be negative seems pretty universal. I do know humans are born sinners—that is why we need God! And our sinful nature can be seen at a young age. My two-year-old, JJ, has a new favorite word, "no," and he likes to yell it at me, his father, or his two big sisters when we do not let him have his way. No one else in the family goes around yelling no with this awful scowl on their faces, but he does, and I think a lot of other two-year-olds do the same thing. It's that sinful nature. They don't call them the terrible twos for nothing! But we're not two and we have a choice. Will we live a glass-half-empty life, always being negative and spewing complaints, or will we live our life with hearts of thankfulness?

As I type these words, I think of the Israelites. As they journeyed from Egypt to the promised land, God was so faithful to them.

He led them out of slavery, parted the Red Sea, sent them manna from the sky, and gave them water in the desert. And yet, it was never enough. After all these blessings, the Israelites—who were never satisfied—went on to say, "If only we had died in Egypt! Or in the wilderness!" (Numbers 14:2). The Israelites missed out on so many blessings because they chose to only focus on their lows instead of being thankful for all God had done for them. As ridiculous and ungrateful as the Israelites seem, I wonder how many times I'm guilty of just that. How many times do we miss out on even more blessings from the Lord because we're being negative Nancies and focusing on what we don't like? Look for the blessings and watch your grumbling turn to gratitude.

PRAYER: Oh Lord, check my heart. May I walk in gratitude and always sing Your praises.

DO THE HARD THING: Let's make a gratitude list. I want you to write out five things that you have to be thankful for, but I want you to think of moments or things that have happened in the past twenty-four hours. Maybe you're thankful for a cool breeze, a big hug from your little one, or that hot cup of coffee in the morning. I strive to make this list every day.

Day 10

RUNNING ON EMPTY

Come to me, all you who are weary and burdened, and I will give you rest. Take my yoke upon you and learn from me, for I am gentle and humble in heart, and you will find rest for your souls. For my yoke is easy and my burden is light."
MATTHEW 11:28-30

I feel like I'm running on empty. My schedule is overflowing, and the to-do list is never ending. As soon as I get caught up with one thing, I'm behind on another. I was late meeting a deadline for work. I forgot about my hair appointment. We're out of milk and basically everything we need for school lunches. To top it all off, the check-engine light in my car has been on for three weeks. I can't keep up; I'm about to throw in the towel.

Do you ever feel like the check-engine light is on in your soul? Life can be hard; it can feel overwhelming. You feel like you're worn down and running on empty, but you feel like you can't stop because everything will fall apart if you do. You try to get it all done by yourself and carry every burden on your own, because at least you know it'll get done. But often, when I start to spiral out of control, it is because I'm trying to shoulder everything on my own. I'm operating out of my own strength, and I was never intended to carry that burden alone.

Jesus tells us that He provides rest for our souls when we bring

Him our burdens. When your check-engine light is on and you're feeling rundown, bring your burdens and your brokenness to the Fixer of all things. He never intended for us to try to walk through this life or carry all these responsibilities by ourselves. So, take a deep breath, my friend, and remember that you were not created to walk or carry your burdens alone.

PRAYER: God, I'm tired of trying to carry all the burdens of life by myself. I try to do everything in my own power, but it just leaves me tired and anxious. Please help me cast all my burdens on You and find rest in Your presence today.

DO THE HARD THING: List some things that have been overwhelming you, then pray over the list and surrender it to the Lord. Yes, those are still responsibilities and duties you have to get done, but lean on the Lord and let Him give you the strength that you need.

_____
_____
_____
_____
_____
_____
_____
_____

Day 11

REJECTION

What, then, shall we say in response to these things? If God is for us, who can be against us? ROMANS 8:31

It hurts to be rejected. Have you ever been fired, cut from a team, dumped, excluded, or uninvited? It can shake your confidence and cause you to question yourself. I remember not being invited to a girls' weekend some of my friends had. I found out about the trip on social media, and the weight of rejection took over my mind and flooded my thoughts. I thought I was friends with these girls! So many of them were flying into town for this, I live one hour away from where the weekend trip was held, and I didn't get the invite? I thought they must all hate me or not want to be around me. I let my mind wander and come up with my own narratives to explain the situation, narratives that could be right or completely wrong.

When we let rejection take over our hearts and minds, we essentially let the Enemy have open access to attack our identity. The fact is, we will continue to face rejection in the future. That's life. So we need a way of guarding our hearts and minds.

We can guard our hearts and minds by remembering there are no perfect people, only a perfect God. Our identity, validation, and worth can only be found in Jesus. You and I will always be invited to His parties. We're welcomed in His throne room. We are invited to draw near; He wants us to always sing and speak His praises. Our heavenly Father will never reject us, overlook us, or leave us out. He will always welcome us with open arms.

PRAYER: Thank You for never forsaking me or rejecting me. Thank You for being for me and not against me! Whenever I face rejection or judgment from others, please remind me of my identity in You. I'm Your child; I'm loved, and I'm chosen.

DO THE HARD THING: Take a few moments and write out a few examples that come to mind of times when you have felt rejected. Now put your hand over the list and pray that the Lord would take away any hurt or pain and say aloud, "I'm chosen, not forsaken; I'm always invited into Your arms."

Day 12

ANCHORED

Then we will no longer be infants, tossed back and forth by the waves, and blown here and there by every wind of teaching and by the cunning and craftiness of people in their deceitful scheming. **EPHESIANS 4:14**

Am I living my life as a Christian in the shallow end, or am I living my life in the deep end? When we first give our lives to the Lord, we're like a small child learning to swim. We stay in the kiddie pool or on the first few steps of the adult pool. We can't yet handle the waves or even getting splashed. But as time goes on, the goal is to learn to swim and navigate deeper waters. No one should stay in the kiddie pool forever. I mean, how silly would it be for me at thirty-six years old to be splashing around in my two-year-old's inflatable pool?

The same is true in our walk with the Lord. First, we accept Jesus into our hearts, then begin to go deeper; and as time goes on, we should grow in our relationship with Him. We move out of the shallow waters and dive deeper with Him.

When we stay in the shallow end, we can falsely believe that we can handle the circumstances of life on our own. We don't need to learn to swim; we're stable and comfortable on the steps! But when the waves come and knock us off our feet, we have trouble keeping our heads above water. When we go deeper with

God in all seasons of life, He prepares us for when the waves and storms come. We'll know He is right beside us, anchoring and protecting us.

We must go out into the depths of the water to be anchored to the Lord. If we want to handle the storms of life and experience all the beauty in the water, we must anchor ourselves to the One who designed and controls the water, the Captain of the sea.

PRAYER: Lord, help me to step out into the depths of the water. I want to go deeper in my relationship with You. Help me to be anchored to You so that no matter what storms come, I won't sink.

DO THE HARD THING: What are some ways you can grow, step out of the kiddie pool, and move to the deep water with Christ? Maybe it's praying for five minutes every day, joining a church, or plugging into a small group. Maybe it's starting a Bible study, reading your Bible more, or surrendering your worries and burdens to Him. Whatever it is, write it out.

_____
_____
_____
_____
_____
_____
_____

Day 13

WHERE IS YOUR FOCUS?

Finally, brothers, whatever is true, whatever is honorable, whatever is just, whatever is pure, whatever is lovely, whatever is commendable, if there is any excellence, if there is anything worthy of praise, think about these things.
PHILIPPIANS 4:8 ESV

Our minds are so very powerful. It is incredible to really look at how what we focus on and think about can affect our lives. Two people can look at the same situation from different lenses and see something completely different. I can look at my kids running around my house, being wild and crazy while I'm trying to get my work done as an annoyance, or I can look at the fact that I have been blessed with children who are healthy, happy, and thriving. Same situation, different lenses.

I remember a few years ago feeling stressed out about my girls arguing like crazy. My daughters are about a year and a half apart, so the closeness in age seemed to induce constant bickering. It felt like all I did was get on to them, correct them, reprimand them. Now, I'm not saying it is wrong to correct them—correction is absolutely necessary—but I was focusing on and making a big deal about every little argument they had. After my husband and I talked, we decided to still correct them but to make a bigger deal about when they got along. We planned to start praising their kindness toward each other, pointing out when they were playing and giggling and getting along. Almost immediately the fighting subsided, and they were getting along more. I believe two things happened:

- I started focusing on the good, therefore I saw more of it. I was not waiting for them to make a mistake and then point it out.
- They started getting more attention for their good behavior, so they began to do more of that.

What you focus on expands into every area of your life, whether you're focusing on your children getting along, your spouse, your workplace, or even your church. We can find good and bad in everyone and everything. I do not know about you, but I want to live a glass-half-full life. I want to have a heart filled with gratitude and praise. We get to decide what we focus on, so let's choose wisely.

PRAYER: God, let my heart be filled with praises today. Help me focus on what is good, true, and lovely.

DO THE HARD THING: Are there any situations you have been looking at through a negative lens? Can you see anything good in that situation? Explain.

Day 14

THE COMPARISON TRAP

I praise you because I am fearfully and wonderfully made; your works are wonderful, I know that full well. **PSALM 139:14**

"How does she have it all together, the perfect home, the perfect spouse, the perfect kids, the perfect vacations—it's just not fair!" Have you ever felt that way when looking at someone else's "perfect" life? If there is one thing that can hold you back from living your life to the fullest and walking in who God has created you to be, it is comparison.

We live in a society where everyone always has their phone on them. A recent study found that on average, we look at our phones 262 times a day—that breaks down to once every five and a half minutes.[1] While we're "checking" our phones, we end up scrolling all the social media sites. I run a social-media-based business, so although I love and appreciate the platform, it can be one of the most fertile breeding grounds for comparison: "She has so many more followers than me. I should be so much further along in my life." And just like that, I can go down this deep, dark rabbit hole of comparison.

We must remind ourselves of a few things when encountering the comparison trap.

1. Everyone shares their highlight reel, so what you're seeing isn't the full reality.

2. You might be comparing your chapter one to someone else's chapter ten. We're all at different stages in life.
3. The girl on Instagram living her best life isn't taking anything away from you. There's not one piece of pie we all have to share; there is enough to go around.

Psalm 139 tells us that we were knitted together by God! We have been fearfully and wonderfully made just the way we are. The Lord has a beautiful plan for you and your life. So stop comparing yourself to others. You have been called to be you and no one else.

PRAYER: As I go about my day and look at the people around me and on my phone screen, I pray that I won't fall into the comparison trap. Instead, I want to focus on Your goodness and the beautiful plan You have for my life.

DO THE HARD THING: Do a little self-reflecting; have you been falling into the comparison trap? What are some ways you can protect your heart and mind so you do not go down that rabbit hole?

Day 15

PROTECT YOUR THOUGHTS

In all these things we are more than conquerors through him who loved us. ROMANS 8:37

Our minds can often feel like battlefields with attacks coming at us from all sides. And this isn't a regular battle. We're fighting against things that feel a lot bigger than us, giants, if you will. The biggest giant of all is anxiety. Anxiety is that intense, excessive, crippling, persistent worry and fear about everything. It can be about those everyday situations, the unknown, the future. Regardless of what brings on those anxious feelings, they can keep you from living your life to the fullest. About 85 percent of the things we worry about never happen.[2] So how can we stop wasting our time on worry and effectively defeat the anxiety giant? We need to remember what the Word of God says in Ephesians 6 and be armed and ready for the battle. Remember, our battle isn't against flesh and blood but against spiritual forces of wickedness in the supernatural.

Ephesians 6:14–17 gives us specific instructions on how to prepare for battle:

> Stand firm then, with the belt of truth buckled around your waist, with the breastplate of righteousness in place, and with your feet fitted with

the readiness that comes from the gospel of peace. In addition to all this, take up the shield of faith, with which you can extinguish all the flaming arrows of the evil one. Take the helmet of salvation and the sword of the Spirit, which is the word of God.

Paul's statement in Ephesians 6:17 is the shortest description given to any of the pieces of armor: "And take up the helmet of salvation." I think that's because there is no explanation needed. The helmet protects against blows to the head, which can be fatal. We must guard our minds so giants like anxiety, worry, and fear can't knock us down. So, sis, it is time to armor up! Yes, there is a battle we have to fight, but we have been given the protection we need. And let's not forget that we're not fighting alone.

PRAYER: Lord, I pray that I would armor up so I can stand my ground when anxiety tries to attack my mind and disrupt my day. Help me remember that You're walking with me through all my battles.

DO THE HARD THING: I challenge you to start praying Ephesians 6:13–17 in the mornings when you wake up. Let's get armored up before we step into battle.

Day 16

PEOPLE DON'T BELONG ON PEDESTALS

God is not man, that he should lie, or a son of man, that he should change his mind. Has he said, and will he not do it? Or has he spoken, and will he not fulfill it? **NUMBERS 23:19 ESV**

I remember hearing the phrase "There are no perfect people, only a perfect God." My initial thought was, *Yeah, yeah I know that.* But I don't often act like I know it. The older I get, the more I find myself let down by people and experiencing that feeling of complete disappointment. Maybe for you it was something a pastor did, or your boss, a leader you admire, a celebrity you fangirl over, or even a spouse. When I'm completely devastated by another person, I pause and ask myself, "Was I placing them on a pedestal?

Early in my marriage, I became so upset if my husband made a mistake or hurt me. I eventually realized I expected him to be perfect. I mean, honestly, the man is pretty amazing, but he will never be perfect; he is human. It was my fault for expecting him to never mess up. I'm not making excuses for when people sin or make mistakes, but so many times when we feel let down by people, we forget they're human.

The Bible is filled with stories of Christ-followers who failed and let other people down. King David, who defeated Goliath, also committed adultery (2 Samuel 11). Peter was a chosen disciple and one of Jesus' closest friends, but he denied knowing Jesus three times (see Luke 22:57). Noah was obedient and built an ark, but he also drank too much wine, and, well, his son found him naked in his tent (see Genesis 9:21). Sarah let her husband, Abraham, sleep with another woman and then hated her for it (see Genesis 16). Moses, who led the Israelites out of captivity, had a temper (see Exodus 2:11-15). Even these spiritual heroes made mistakes.

Realizing that people are imperfect does not make it any less painful or wrong for people to let you down and hurt you, but the truth is that it is bound to happen over and over. The closer you get to people, the higher the chances are that they will fail you. So let's remember to put our hope and trust in the One who is never failing and always faithful.

PRAYER: Lord, I pray that I would keep You and only You on the pedestal of my life. Help me to put my hope and complete trust in You above all else. Thank You for Your faithfulness and for never failing me.

DO THE HARD THING: Have you been hurt recently by someone? Were you placing them on a pedestal? Are there people in your life you need to take off a pedestal?

Day 17

STRENGTHS AND WEAKNESSES

But he said to me, "My grace is sufficient for you, for my power is made perfect in weakness." Therefore I will boast all the more gladly about my weakness, so that Christ's power may rest on me. 2 CORINTHIANS 12:9

In job interviews, most interviewers will ask about your strengths and weaknesses. I think it's so funny that everyone's advice is to say weaknesses that seem like strengths: "I'm a little too self-sufficient," or "I'm too perfectionistic," or "I focus too much on the details." Translation: I'm an independent, hard worker who will get things done with excellence.

God isn't an interviewer though. When we're weak and we feel that our weaknesses are getting the better of us, we can bring everything to Him. He will walk alongside us and give us strength in our shortcomings. We weren't created to do life alone. If we could handle it all—if we were enough alone—then our human selves wouldn't think that we needed God. So, if you feel weak, not enough, and tired—good!

Second Corinthians 12:9 says plain and clear that "'My grace is all you need. My power works best in weakness.' So now I'm glad to boast about my weaknesses, so that the power of Christ can work through me" (NLT). His power shows up best when we're weak, because then we know our strength does not come from within us but from Christ's power. Billy Graham put it best when he said, "When we come to the end of ourselves, we come to the beginning of God."[3]

When I operate out of my own strength, I fail every time. But when I acknowledge that the Lord's power is made perfect in my weakness and I rely on my heavenly Father to help me, I'm more than able. Acknowledge that you can't carry everything this life throws at you alone. Acknowledge the weaknesses that you might be trying to disguise as strengths. Hand over your burdens, worries, everything you have been trying to do, and navigate alone to the Lord. Lean into His strength and find rest in His arms.

PRAYER: God, I feel weak today. Please walk alongside me. Thank You for Your never-ending grace that provides me with strength.

DO THE HARD THING: In what areas of your life have you been walking alone? Write out some things, people, or situations you need to fully give to the Lord.

Day 18

NO SUCH THING AS AN ORDINARY MASTERPIECE

For we are God's masterpiece. He has created us anew in Christ Jesus, so we can do the good things he planned for us long ago. EPHESIANS 2:10

Sometimes I have days or weeks when I don't feel special, when everything about me seems ordinary and plain. I feel like I just blend in and don't stand out. I see so many people around me with amazing gifts and talents, and I'll catch myself thinking, *But what about me? Did God forget to include those when He designed me?*

I think we have all thrown ourselves a pity party a time or two. Feeling less than or ordinary is a lie from the Enemy. If you're living and breathing, then you're a uniquely designed masterpiece created by God. Ephesians 2:10 clearly states that not only are you a masterpiece, but God has also planned "good things" for you. Yes, you! And these things were planned in advance for you, sister. You're not forgotten; you're so very special to your heavenly Father.

I always think about how much I love each of my three children uniquely, not one more than the other, but they each have a special place in my heart. Our Father loves us so much more than we could ever comprehend. He knitted us together before we were born, He numbered the hairs on our head, and He even recorded every day of our lives in advance. Do not listen to the lies from the Enemy: you're cared for, loved, and a one-of-a-kind masterpiece designed by the Creator of the universe. There's no such thing as an ordinary masterpiece.

PRAYER: God, help me see myself through Your eyes today. I pray that I would learn to view myself as a masterpiece You handcrafted for the purpose of Your kingdom.

DO THE HARD THING: Ask the Lord to show you some of the strengths and talents He has given you. It is so easy to focus on what we feel we lack but we can't neglect the gifts He has given to us.

Day 19

LIVING FOR ETERNITY

Set your minds on things above, not on earthly things.
COLOSSIANS 3:2

I often become caught up in things that honestly don't matter: not getting invited to something, being envious of something someone else has, or not being asked to speak at a work event. Have you ever caught yourself obsessing over things that seem important in the moment but if you zoom out and really look at them from a bird's-eye view, they're trivial? I am not saying you shouldn't ever feel hurt or frustrated; those feelings are normal and valid. But every now and then—okay, actually, every day—I have to remind myself that I need to live my life with eternity in mind.

My mission statement for my life is to know God and make Him known. I want everything I spend time on to either help me know God better or help others come to know Him. I have learned that when I shift my thinking to knowing God and making Him known, the trivial things don't matter quite as much. I can bounce back from not being invited to this or that or feeling overlooked at my job. Am I pointing people to Jesus? Yes. That right there is all that really matters.

I love the mission statement God gives us in Mark 16:15: "He said to them, 'Go into all the world and preach the gospel to all creation.'" That is our job; that is what believers have been called to do. Every day, I pray that my focus would be on this and this alone. All that really matters is that when I stand before the Lord on judgment day, He says, "Well done, my good and faithful servant" (Matthew 25:21 NLT). Let this be your reminder to focus on those things with an eternal value and let go of the ones that do not really matter.

PRAYER: Help me focus on You and see the world and my life with an eternal perspective. May I live to know You and make You known today.

DO THE HARD THING: Do a little self-reflection. Have you been preoccupied and focused on things that have an earthly value or an eternal value?

Day 20

LET GO OF THE WHEEL, SIS

Trust in the LORD with all your heart, And lean not on your own understanding; In all your ways acknowledge Him, And He shall direct your paths. **PROVERBS 3:5-6 NKJV**

Have you ever felt like you were at a crossroads, wondering which way to go and stressed because you're the one having to navigate your life? Maybe you've thought, *What if I make a wrong turn? What if I crash?*

Let me tell you a little secret: we don't feel equipped in the driver's seat because we were not created to be the driver. It can be hard to relinquish control of the wheel, especially if you're a control freak like me. I constantly try to take the wheel of my life and be in control but that usually results in me stalling, crashing, or ending up on the side of the road with a flat tire. And let's be honest, it's exhausting and tiring always having to navigate.

Occasionally, we invite God to sit in the back, and sometimes we even invite Him to ride shotgun, but you know what? We need to pull the car over, hand over the keys, and let Him take the wheel instead! You do not have to drive alone. In fact, why not relinquish control to the chief navigator? Isn't it so much more relaxing to let go and enjoy the ride? Psalm 46:10 says, "Stop striving and know that I am God" (NASB). In the original Hebrew language, the phrase "stop striving" indicates giving up by letting our hands down.[4] Wow! You see, there is no way to hold the steering wheel and allow God to drive at the same time. It is time to let go of the wheel, sis.

PRAYER: Jesus, take the wheel. I'm letting You drive today. I pray that I would let You have full control and not try to take it back. Thank You for directing my paths.

DO THE HARD THING: Ask yourself who is in the driver seat of your life right now. Have you invited the Lord to be in the car? Is He in the back seat? Is He riding shotgun? Or is He in His rightful place, driving?

Day 21

FAIL FORWARD

Though a righteous person falls seven times, he will get up, but the wicked will stumble into ruin. PROVERBS 24:16 CSB

Have you ever failed and blown it big-time? Have you ever felt unworthy of God's grace and mercy? Have you ever made a promise that you would do better only to find yourself making yet another mistake? If you have failed—join the club.

If you dive into the greatest Book of all time, you'll find story after story of godly men and women who also made mistakes and failed, despite their love for God. Sarah laughed at God's promise that she would bear children and then denied she laughed, as if God wouldn't know. Saul killed Christians, Jonah ran from God, Gideon was fearful, Rahab was a prostitute, Samson was immoral, and that's just a small selection!

And yet, Sarah became the mother of the nation of Israel. Saul (known also as the apostle Paul) went on to write thirteen books of the Bible. Jonah went to Nineveh and convinced the entire city to repent. Gideon led an army of three hundred to victory. Rahab helped the Israelites defeat Jericho. And Samson was given strength one last time to judge the Philistines.

They made mistakes and failed, yet they still went on to do great things for the kingdom of God. God's grace is available to us because Jesus paid the price for our sins. We may not deserve grace, but God gives it to us freely. So, get back up, dust yourself off, let it be a lesson learned, and keep moving forward.

PRAYER: God, please help me see myself as more than my mistakes. Thank You for always being there when I fall to help me up.

DO THE HARD THING: You may have fallen, but how can you use that mistake to learn and move forward?

Day 22

RIGHT NOW

"For my thoughts are not your thoughts, neither are your ways my ways," declares the LORD. "As the heavens are higher than the earth, so are my ways higher than your ways and my thoughts than your thoughts." ISAIAH 55:8-9

Have you ever wanted something right now? That dream that's on your heart that you have been working so hard for, wondering when it might come to fruition. That healing you have been praying for, wondering why God hasn't answered it yet. That blessing you have been hoping for, wondering where it is. Waiting is hard. I've heard it said before that we need to fall in love with the process, not the outcome. We have to start asking ourselves, *What is the Lord teaching me or showing me, or how is He growing me during the wait?*

God's ways and His thoughts are higher than our ways and thoughts. We see a small glimpse while God sees the full picture. We have to trust our heavenly Father and His timing, because we ultimately want to win for a lifetime, not just a moment. Regardless of what your situation looks or feels like today, God somehow, some way works all things together for good.

PRAYER: Waiting is hard. I don't like it, but I know You're teaching me and growing me through the process. Help me see the beauty even here and not just look toward the outcome. Help me trust Your timing.

DO THE HARD THING: Write out some things you're currently waiting for. Then decide to trust the Lord and His perfect timing, praying specifically over what you're waiting for.

Day 23

FRIENDSHIP

As iron sharpens iron, so one person sharpens another.
PROVERBS 27:17

"Okay, so I give up. Having girlfriends isn't for me! I just don't get along with girls; drama is always involved. I spend time investing with a friend and then I get hurt. I feel like I can never quite fit in with any group. It stinks to feel excluded. And I don't have time to build friendships in this season of my life."

Have you ever had one or all of those thoughts go through your head? The Enemy, Satan, has been after females since the beginning of time. He targeted Eve and tempted her first (see Genesis 3:1-6). Then there were the two women both claiming to be mother to the same baby (see 1 Kings 3:16-28). And the huge argument between two women, Euodia and Syntyche, who helped spread the gospel in Phillipi—even Paul got involved and urged them to come to peace and end their squabble (see Philippians 4:2-3). And there was even a little drama when Martha threw Mary under the bus for not helping her (see Luke 10:38-42). I think the Enemy targets female relationships because women in healthy relationships and friendships are powerful.

Friendships are hard, and yes, you'll most likely get hurt or hurt someone, because we're human. And yes, it takes time and effort to build good friendships. But I have learned that an iron-sharpens-iron friendship is worth the time and effort. The benefit and beauty that come from friendships will always outweigh the risk. The Bible tells us in Ecclesiastes 4:9-10, "Two people are better off than one, for they can help each other succeed. If one person falls, the other can reach out and help. But someone who falls alone is in real trouble" (NLT). When we find friends who help us succeed, sharpen us and make us better, and help us up when we fall, we'll experience friendship as God intended. Take the time to nurture and grow friendships that sharpen you and leave you feeling encouraged, inspired, and filled up. And be sure to be that type of friend to the women who are in your circle.

PRAYER: God, please help me find friends who sharpen me and to be a friend who sharpens others. I pray that I would honor You in all my friendships.

DO THE HARD THING: Name a few friends who truly sharpen you and then commit to make time to continue to grow those friendships. If no names come to mind, begin praying that the Lord would bring a friend into your life who will stick closer than a sister.

Day 24

MUSTARD SEEDS

Now faith is confidence in what we hope for and assurance about what we do not see. HEBREWS 11:1

Sometimes I struggle to believe. I want to believe for healing, believe that my loved one will come to know Jesus, believe that my dream will come to pass—but doubt creeps in. I begin to lose faith. I want to believe, but it's as if I don't know how.

In these moments I stop and pray three simple words: "increase my faith." I find myself praying this often. Each time I call on the Lord and ask for faith to believe, I know He hears me. I have a mustard seed keychain, and every time I pick up my keys or look down at it while I'm driving, I focus on Matthew 17:20: "'You don't have enough faith,' Jesus told them. 'I tell you the truth, if you had faith even as small as a mustard seed, you could say to this mountain, "Move from here to there," and it would move. Nothing would be impossible'" (NLT). I may not have faith the size of a mountain, but I know I can muster up faith the size of that teeny tiny mustard seed.

PRAYER: Lord, give me the faith Noah had to build that ark, the faith Moses had to stand up against Pharaoh, and the faith David had to face a giant with nothing but a sling and rock. Increase my faith to be like the faith the blind man had to see and the faith the bleeding woman had to be healed by just touching the hem of Jesus' robe. I want to live my life with those kinds of faith!

DO THE HARD THING: Write out some areas in your life where you need to ask the Lord to increase your faith.

Day 25

OUT WITH THE OLD, IN WITH THE NEW

Forget the former things; do not dwell on the past. See, I am doing a new thing! ISAIAH 43:18-19

The past. Those two simple words can bring an onslaught of memories and regrets. I believe one of the greatest ways the Enemy distracts us is by reminding us of our past. These memories can fill us with feelings of shame, unworthiness, and guilt. If the Enemy can't destroy you, he will distract you. Distractions are designed to get you off course. If we're constantly looking back, how can we look forward and keep our eyes on the Lord and the plans He has for our future?

When I think of someone with a messy past, I think of Mary Magdalene. She was once possessed by seven demons, but when Jesus freed her, she followed Him for the rest of her life and even funded His ministry! If she had held onto her past, she would have potentially missed and counted herself out of opportunities to further God's kingdom. What a tragedy that would have been! Your past can only hold you captive if you haven't surrendered it to God.

The Bible tells us that we're "new creation[s]. The old has passed away; behold, the new has come" (2 Corinthians 5:17 ESV). Forget the former things; God is doing a new thing! Can you see it? Do you feel it? He is restoring what is broken and providing water in the wilderness.

PRAYER: Lord, I surrender my past to You today. Help me not to dwell on it, even as the Enemy tries to distract me. Thank You for making me a new creation and for having a plan for my future filled with hope and purpose.

DO THE HARD THING: What mistakes or regrets do you have that you need to release to God and receive His never-ending grace?

Day 26

FORGIVENESS

Make allowance for each other's faults, and forgive anyone who offends you. Remember, the Lord forgave you, so you must forgive others. COLOSSIANS 3:13 NLT

Forgiving someone who hurt you is tough. It is easy to remember the pain they caused. Broken trust is so hard to rebuild. Forgiving what someone did to you does not mean that what they did was okay! Forgiveness frees you and allows you to move forward with your life and the goodness the Lord has in store for you. You're not forgiving just for their benefit but for yours as well.

We need the Holy Spirit to take over our heart and mind to help us forgive as Christ forgave. When I struggle with forgiving and letting go, I remember what Jesus said as He hung on that cross, watching the soldiers gamble for His clothes: "Father, forgive them, for they don't know what they are doing" (Luke 23:34 NLT). When we truly forgive those who hurt us, we can experience God's forgiveness more fully, and we aren't burdened with grudges, bitterness, resentment, or hard feelings that weigh heavy on our souls. If someone severely hurt you, do not let them rob you of anything else; they have taken enough, and it is time to fully forgive so you can live a life of freedom. It is important to remember that forgiveness isn't a suggestion but a commandment.

Jesus gives us an example in the parable of the unmerciful servant in Matthew 18:21-35. In that story a servant borrowed ten thousand bags of gold from his master and couldn't pay it back. The master forgave him and canceled his debt. But then the servant whose debt was canceled couldn't forgive another servant who owed him a hundred silver coins. When the master heard about what had happened, he was furious. He had the unmerciful servant punished for not having the same mercy in his heart that the master had demonstrated. In this parable, Jesus showed us that no matter how great the offense is or how often someone hurts us, God expects us to forgive them the same way He forgives us time and time again.

PRAYER: Thank You for forgiving all my sins. I pray that I would be able to extend the same forgiveness to those who hurt me.

DO THE HARD THING: Is there someone (or many people) you need to forgive? Forgiving them does not make what they did right, and you may need to set boundaries or not have them in your life at all. Regardless, you have to forgive them so you can release what was done and move forward without holding onto the offense(s).

Day 27

FEELING ALONE

The LORD is near to all who call on him, to all who call on him in truth. He fulfills the desires of those who fear him; he hears their cry and saves them. **PSALM 145:18-19**

We've all felt lonely from time to time, and the COVID-19 pandemic really took feelings of loneliness and isolation up a level (or ten). During those times when we feel isolated, the Enemy tends to work overtime in messing with our heads. The truth, no matter what lie you may have been listening to, is that you're never alone. The Creator of the heavens and earth, the One who painted the sunsets and with one word spoke the oceans and mountains into existence, desires a relationship with you. Let that sink in. He is with you, He loves you, and He wants a relationship with you. We're promised in James 4:8 that when we draw near to God, He will draw near to us.

Our heavenly Father cares about our feelings, our problems, and everything we face, big and small. Jesus came to this earth in the form of a human and experienced many of the feelings we feel. He faced rejection and was abandoned by friends. His disciples even fell asleep while He was praying just a day before He was crucified. That would make me feel like I was walking through something completely alone. But Jesus knew God was always near.

Whether you're in a crowded room feeling alone, isolated in your home without a person to talk to, or feeling left out or forgotten, you have a Father who is right by your side and will never ever leave you or forsake you. Take a moment and call out and draw near to Him.

PRAYER: God, thank You for always being near and walking with me through life. I confess that I've felt lonely lately, but I know that with You, I'm never truly alone. Please help me feel Your presence today.

DO THE HARD THING: Next time you feel lonely, call out to God instead of trying to distract yourself. When we draw near to Him, He draws near to us. Sometimes our loneliness brings us closer to God.

Day 28

THE GREAT DEFENDER

The LORD is my protector; he is my strong fortress. My God is my protection, and with him I am safe. He protects me like a shield; he defends me and keeps me safe. **PSALM 18:2 GNT**

Sometimes when I read a scathing comment under one of my Instagram posts or figure out someone was talking about me behind my back, I feel so frustrated and misunderstood. It doesn't feel good when people are saying untrue things, my words are getting twisted around, or I'm just flat out being hated on.

Am I supposed to let people criticize me and speak untruths? The truth is that there will always be people in your life (or on social media) who misunderstand you, criticize you, hate on you, judge you, attack you, spread rumors about you, and flat out don't like you. In these moments, it's helpful to remember that even Jesus had haters. Jesus experienced all these things and more. When I'm criticized, my human nature wants to criticize back. When I feel attacked, I want to fight back. When I'm misunderstood, I want to defend myself. But then I remind myself of how Jesus responded: with grace. Every single time.

It isn't our job to defend, fight back, or be on guard to protect ourselves. It can be hard not to slip into defense mode, but if you think about it, how liberating and freeing is it that we do not have to carry the weight of constantly defending ourselves? In 1 Peter

2:23, we're told that even Jesus didn't fight back: "When they hurled their insults at him, he did not retaliate; when he suffered, he made no threats. Instead, he entrusted himself to him who judges justly." He let God be the ultimate judge and defender. We have a heavenly Father who is the ultimate defender and protector of His children. And you know what? I know without a shadow of a doubt that He is a much better defender than you or I could ever be.

PRAYER: God, I confess that sometimes I want to fight fire with fire. I have the perfect comeback to the snarky comment someone made. But You call me higher. Help me respond to the haters with grace and love like Jesus did. Thank You for being my great defender. Amen.

DO THE HARD THING: What are some situations where you've felt criticized or misunderstood that you need to just let go and let God be in control? Surrender those to Him today.

_____
_____
_____
_____
_____
_____
_____

Day 29

POURING FROM AN EMPTY CUP

He gives strength to the weary and increases the power of the weak. ISAIAH 40:29

For most of my life, I have preached that you can't pour from an empty cup. A pitcher can't be filled up if it remains in the "pour position." You must be filled up to pour out. While I still see truth in the idea that you want to stay filled up so you can pour out, I also know it's not always possible. Most likely there will be times (many times) in life when we're empty, drained, and at our wits' end. If you're a mama like me, there is no pause or time out. Momming is a 24/7 thing. We still have to keep pouring whether we feel filled up or not.

I can think of one of my hardest seasons in life when my husband worked a ton. He was an equity trader full-time, and he always had after-work dinners, meetings, travel, and so on. Plus, he was the young adults/associate pastor at our church, which meant evening services, Sunday services, staff meetings, and more. We had two babies under the age of two. During this time, I took care of the kids, ran the women's ministry at our church, and was starting my own business. I felt like I was juggling one too many things by myself and that my pitcher was empty more often than not. I didn't always have time to be filled up between all my responsibilities.

I don't know what season of life you're in—maybe you're juggling school, or multiple jobs, young babies, kids with seventy-three after school activities, or teenagers. And while I agree it is much better to pour from a filled pitcher, we can still find hope and strength in the times when we're empty. In those hard times—the seasons where you have nothing left to pour out—you don't have to panic. God's power works best then. There's no way we can take credit for anything because the strength we receive to get through the day is from Him. The extra dose of patience we get to deal with the teething baby is from Him. The rest we feel when we didn't get any sleep because we were up all night with our toddler comes from Him too. The times when we're empty help us recognize who holds us up in times of difficulty or adversity. Although I like when I'm able to check off all the self-care boxes and stay filled-up, even in my hot-mess struggle-bus moments I can still pour out into my three babies, my husband, that friend who needs me, and into my team because the Lord's power is made perfect in my weakness.

PRAYER: My cup feels empty today, God. Please provide me with Your strength to be Your hands and feet today.

DO THE HARD THING: Ask God specifically for what you need to get through the day.

Day 30

YOU'RE NOT FORGOTTEN

You are the God who sees me ... I have now seen the one who sees me." **GENESIS 16:13**

Do you ever feel like everyone else is getting their promises, blessings, and answered prayers while you feel like you're left on the sidelines? Forgotten. Overlooked. Invisible.

When I think about feeling overlooked, I think of Hagar from the Bible. Hagar was Sarah's Egyptian slave. Before Sarah and Abraham had kids, Sarah came up with an idea to have Hagar sleep with her husband to ensure a bloodline continued. When Hagar got pregnant, Sarah resented her and treated her so harshly that Hagar fled into the desert. God in His faithfulness saw Hagar and met her in the desert. God loved her and cared about her. He told her that He would multiply her offspring and that she should name her son (Ishmael). In Genesis 16:13 Hagar said, "You are the God who sees me … I have now seen the One who sees me." I think it's safe to assume that Hagar had heard much about God from Abraham and Sarah. But until that desert encounter, He was "their God." But after meeting her in the desert, He showed Hagar that He could be her God as well. She went from hearing about Him to seeing Him herself.

If you feel like you're in a wilderness season where you feel forgotten and overlooked, I encourage you to seek God with eyes wide open. You, my friend, are never alone. We serve a God who is always faithful to meet us right where we are. No matter who you are or where you are, the Lord sees you, loves you, and cares for you.

PRAYER: Lord, please open my eyes to Your presence and goodness today. I feel like I'm walking through the wilderness alone, and I would love to see You working in me and through me in this season. Thank You for loving me and never abandoning me. You are my God.

DO THE HARD THING: Have you ever felt forgotten, alone, or abandoned? Maybe you feel it right now. Take a moment to write down how you are feeling and then try talking to someone you trust about the season you are in.

Day 31

A PROMISE DELAYED

But if we look forward to something we don't yet have, we must wait patiently and confidently. ROMANS 8:25 NLT

Has there ever been something you felt like the Lord promised you but it hasn't come to fruition? Have you ever wanted something so badly but it is nowhere in sight? Have you ever had a dream but doubted it could become a reality?

When I think of waiting on a promise, my mind goes to Hannah and her ache, longing for a child. Hannah not only had to deal with the hopes and letdowns of not having a baby, but her husband, Elkanah, had another wife, Peninnah, who was able to bear children and would tease and mock Hannah constantly. But as Hannah waited, she continued to cry out in prayer and plead with God to grant her a child. He answered her prayer and Hannah was blessed with a son, Samuel. Hannah had promised to dedicate Samuel to the Lord, and she kept that promise. I don't know why Hannah had to wait for years. God's timing is truly a mystery. But what I do know is that God heard Hannah's prayers, saw her dedication and fervor, and answered her pleas.

When doubt creeps in and that desire, dream, or promise begins to seem impossible, we can stand on the promise that we're given in Matthew 7:7-8: "Ask and it will be given to you; seek and you will find; knock and the door will be opened to you. For everyone who asks receives; the one who seeks finds; and to the one who knocks, the door will be opened." If you're in a waiting season, I want you to go boldly to the throne room of God and ask, pray, praise, and plead as Hannah did. Prayer moves the hand of God.

PRAYER: God, You know the desires and dreams in my heart. If they're not from You, please remove them; if they're from You, give me patience as I expectantly wait for You to fulfill them.

DO THE HARD THING: Have you been praying for something and feel like it has been delayed? I want you to commit to fervently praying for whatever it is on your heart.

Day 32

INNER CIRCLE

Friends come and friends go, but a true friend sticks by you like family. **PROVERBS 18:24 MSG**

We all have circles of friends. Most of us have many circles of friends—our work friends, school friends, church friends, college friends. And then there is your inner circle, the ones you spend the most time with and allow into your life and they allow you into theirs. Every so often, you want to look around and see who you have in your circle. Are these transactional relationships, or are these transformational relationships?

Transactional relationships are when they profit from knowing you; when they gain, take, and get what they desire. They can be opportunists, the ones who are close when you're on top but are nowhere to be seen when things get tough. These people want to be in the Instagram photo and invited to all the events, but they don't want to be there when you're crying on the couch after receiving bad news. They do not want to truly be in your life or a part of the behind-the-scenes.

Transformational relationships are those iron-sharpens-iron ones. When iron rubs together, it is sharpened. If iron grates against something weak, what happens to the iron? It either destroys the other material or becomes dull. In transformational relationships, both people give and take. They both offer accountability and bring wisdom and strength. They don't compete but instead inspire each other. They're there with you in the highs and lows.

Not everyone is in your corner. They may be in the room, but it doesn't take long for them to run out the door. But those in your corner, those are the transformational friends who stick by you like family. Having an inner circle isn't exclusionary: it just means you don't share all parts of your life with everyone you meet. Having an inner circle allows you to better protect your time, energy, and heart. Not everyone is a transformational friend, so evaluate who you have let into your inner circle. Even Jesus had an inner circle. Jesus had His twelve disciples and then there was His inner circle: Peter, James, and John. Let the Lord show you who those iron-sharpens-iron people are in your room. And be sure to invest in them as they invest back into you.

PRAYER: I pray that You would show me the people who are in my corner, my transformational friends. Help me invest in them as they invest in me.

DO THE HARD THING: Who are some friends that come to mind when you think of those who are in your corner, in your inner circle? If no one comes to mind, think about some ways you can connect with other women. Could you join a Bible study, MOPs group, small group at church? Is there someone you have been wanting to get to know you could invite to coffee?

Day 33

PRAY CONTINUALLY

Rejoice always, pray continually, give thanks in all circumstances; for this is God's will for you in Christ Jesus.
1 THESSALONIANS 5:16-18

Have you ever paused and realized that your prayer life consists of thanking God for your meals before you eat and then maybe a bedtime prayer with your kids? I can think of many times in my life when prayer became more of a routine than being part of a close relationship where I talked to my Creator. I have no doubt that the Lord wants to be in constant communication with His children. He wants to not only be with us but to also talk with us and walk with us throughout the day. He wants to speak to us, and He wants our relationship to grow closer and deeper.

Prayer is one of the most powerful tools we have for spiritual warfare. Ephesians 6:12 tells us that "We are not fighting against humans. We are fighting against forces and authorities and against rulers of darkness and powers in the spiritual world" (CEV). If you read on in verse 18, we're told to "Never stop praying, especially for others. Always pray by the power of the Spirit. Stay alert and keep praying for God's people." Paul does not say to pray before we eat, before bed, or when we need something; he says to always pray.

Just like I long to have a close relationship and always talk to my children, the Lord desires that with us even more. Talk to Jesus as you go through your day. Stop and pray for your spouse, children, or that friend the Lord laid on your heart; pray for our country, the world, your pastor, or the woman you passed in the grocery store that the Holy Spirit pointed out to you; and even pray for your enemies, or the person who hurt you and caused you pain. Prayer can be in the morning when you have your coffee, in the school pick-up line, or when you wake up in the middle of the night. There is no right or wrong way to talk to Jesus if it's done reverently. Just as we breathe, we should pray.

PRAYER: What things on your heart do you need to pray about? Take a moment and talk to God about those things now.

DO THE HARD THING: Praying continually doesn't mean you're constantly walking around with your eyes closed but that you approach life with an attitude of humble submission to God. Write out the ways you need to humbly submit to God and commit to doing so this week.

Day 34

ASKING OUR FATHER

Jabez cried out to the God of Israel, "Oh, that you would bless me and enlarge my territory! Let your hand be with me, and keep me from harm so that I will be free from pain." And God granted his request. 1 CHRONICLES 4:10

Have you ever felt guilty asking God for things? I believe Christians sometimes think we can't ask our Father for blessings, favor, promotions, or things. It is as though we're un-Christian or selfish to ask. I don't know about you, but I love to bless my children. Now, there are times they may ask for things I know wouldn't be good for them, so I do not grant those requests. But it makes my heart happy to be able to do things for them that they desire.

God isn't a genie here to grant our every wish. But time and time again we are told to ask: "Therefore I tell you, whatever you ask for in prayer, believe that you have received it, and it will be yours" (Mark 11:24); "If you believe, you will receive whatever you ask for in prayer" (Matthew 21:22); "You ask and do not receive, because you ask wrongly, to spend it on your passions" (James 4:3 ESV). These Scriptures show me that, yes, I do want to ask my Father for those desires on my heart, because when we delight ourselves in the Lord, He does give us the desires of our heart. But Scripture also reminds me to check my motives in every request I take to the Lord.

In *The Prayer of Jabez*, Bruce Wilkinson tells a story about a man who goes to heaven and sees a warehouse with boxes stacked from the floor to the ceiling. In the boxes were tons and tons of blessings. They were blessings God had given His children, but they never opened them to use them. When I read this story, I started thinking about what blessings God has put on my path that I've missed out on. Maybe some were for me and my family, but what about the opportunities God gave me to bless others? Blessings are bidirectional. I know I feel even more blessed when I give than when I receive. My point is this: I don't want to leave any blessing unopened for myself or with which I can bless others. The Lord wants to bless His children, so go to Him boldly in prayer and petition.

PRAYER: God, I want everything You have for me, and I don't want anything You don't have for me. Help me to boldly ask for and embrace the blessings You give me for me and to use to bless others.

DO THE HARD THING: Make a list of desires you want to ask the Lord for.

Day 35

FROM BITTER TO BLESSED

The LORD is close to the brokenhearted and saves those who are crushed in spirit. **PSALM 34:19**

Have you ever felt disappointed in God? If you have, you aren't alone. I can remember feeling so very disappointed when I lost my father at twenty-two years old. It was an unexpected, devastating tragedy. My mom was left a widow and had to raise two of my younger siblings on her own. I didn't understand why it happened; I still don't. Feelings of disappointment will come, but it is what we decide to do with those feelings that matters.

When I think of people from the Bible who had to walk through disappointment, I think of Naomi. In Ruth 1:20-21, Naomi said, "'Don't call me Naomi' … 'Instead, call me Mara, for the Almighty has made life very bitter for me. I went away full, but the LORD has brought me home empty'" (NLT). To say Naomi was disappointed was an understatement. The name Naomi means "pleasant" or "delightful," but after losing not only her husband but both of her sons, she said "call me Mara," which means "bitter." I can't imagine what it would have felt like for Naomi to lose her husband and both sons—the ones who protected and provided for her. But this story didn't end in tragedy. Ruth, Naomi's daughter-in-law, stayed with her and refused to leave her side. Ruth ended up marrying Boaz (thanks to Naomi's help), and Naomi ended up becoming the nurse for Ruth's son. The child went on to be the grandfather of King David and the many-times great-grandfather of Jesus. Naomi went from bitter to blessed.

When we're disappointed, we want to disconnect from God, but that's the worst thing we can do. It's during those hard times when we feel let down, hurt, and forgotten that we need to turn to God. We need to connect to the Source of healing. When we take our disappointments to the Lord, it can lead to a divine appointment. Let God meet you and minister to you even in your frustration. Jesus knows exactly what we need, and there is always hope.

PRAYER: Lord, help me bring all my disappointments before You today. Help me trust that You have good things in store for me.

DO THE HARD THING: What are some things that have disappointed you? Write them out and lay them at the feet of Jesus. Trust that He will be faithful to work all things together for good.

Day 36

DREAMER & DOER

Before I made you in your mother's womb, I chose you. Before you were born, I set you apart for a special work.
JEREMIAH 1:5 NCV

Pause and think about some of the dreams in your heart. I truly believe those dreams are deposited into our hearts by our Creator. They were put there for a reason and for such a time as this. You absolutely have a beautiful, special work God designed just for you.

You have the dreams, but maybe they have been pushed to the back burner. Maybe they have been tucked away or maybe you're too scared to step out and get started. You see, having the dream is part one. But part two is making the decision to pursue it. You can have all the dreams in the world, you can talk about them, think about them, and wish for them, but if you do not take action, you'll stay a dreamer.

Deuteronomy 28:8 talks about the Lord blessing everything we put our hands to, but the key is that your hands must be doing something. How can the Lord bless you as you pursue that dream or step into your calling without you first deciding to be a doer and apply action? So, yes, let's dream crazy big God-sized dreams, and then let's also be confident enough to step out in faith and pursue them. Let us trust that the One who gave us those dreams will equip us with everything we need to see them come into existence.

PRAYER: Thank You for the dreams You've placed on my heart and for equipping me with everything I need to chase after them. I pray that I would take a bold step toward my dreams today, knowing You are with me.

DO THE HARD THING: What are some dreams that have been on your heart that you know you need to step out and pursue?

Day 37

PEOPLE PLEASING

For we speak as messengers approved by God to be entrusted with the Good News. Our purpose is to please God, not people. He alone examines the motives of our hearts.
1 THESSALONIANS 2:4 NLT

Hi, I'm SheriLynn, and I'm a people pleaser. I know I'm not the only one. We all want people to like us, and most of us don't want to do anything that will make waves. But I want you to hear this loud and clear: You can't follow Jesus and not make any waves. He calls us to wake people up, to meet with sinners, to pray big, bold prayers—those things will cause some waves.

We're not on this earth to please other people; we're on this earth to honor God and make His name known. Jesus is the perfect example of this; He was a wave-maker who was always more concerned with pleasing God than pleasing other people. He flipped over tables, called people out, rebuked demons, raised the dead—all in the name of God and for the purpose of pleasing Him. He was not afraid of confrontation when it meant making God's name known.

Do you spend more of your day thinking about ways you can please God or the people around you? Honestly, I spend more time thinking about pleasing others. To combat this, we need to fill our minds and hearts with God's Word—meditate on His messages for us—and learn a thing or two from Jesus' example.

PRAYER: Lord, I pray that I would be able to focus on pleasing You today and not worry so much about pleasing other people. Help me make Your name known and follow Your Spirit guiding me.

DO THE HARD THING: Is there an area of your life where you feel like God may be calling you to do something that would make some waves? Maybe it's asking a stranger how you can be praying for them. Maybe it's starting a Bible study. Or maybe it's standing up for yourself at work. Whatever it is, remember that you're on this earth to please God, not people.

Day 38

ALTOGETHER LOVABLE

I am convinced that neither death nor life, neither angels nor demons, neither the present nor the future, nor any powers, neither height nor depth, nor anything else in all creation, will be able to separate us from the love of God that is in Christ Jesus our Lord. **ROMANS 8:38-39**

Do you ever have those days when you feel completely unlovable? On those tough days, our self-esteem really takes a hit. The truth is that you and I are not unlovable; we're never unlovable. We can't do anything, say anything, or think anything that would ever make us unlovable to God. Nothing can separate us from His love.

You know when you had your first crush and you thought it would last forever? Then, by the time the next school year rolled around, you already had a different crush (or two)? Yeah, God's love isn't like that; it's pretty much the opposite. God's love is enduring, everlasting, unconditional, perfect, and incorruptible. When we live from a place of deeply understanding God's everlasting love for us, we begin to live lives full of praise and gratitude, magnifying His goodness. We can never fully understand God's love for us on this side of heaven, but the more time we spend with Him, the more we experience His love and the more we're able to extend that unconditional love to others.

In John 13:35, Jesus said, "By this everyone will know that you are my disciples, if you love one another." When we view ourselves through the lens of God's enduring love for us, we can't help but extend that love to those around us. You, my friend, are not unlovable but deeply loved by your Creator.

PRAYER: God, help me understand more of Your love for me today. I don't feel lovable, but I know You love me and that Your love for me is everlasting. I pray that I would feel Your love all around me today and be able to extend that same love to others.

DO THE HARD THING: Next time you look in the mirror or make a mistake and have a negative thought about yourself, say aloud, "Nothing can separate me from God's love." Take a moment to rest in the knowledge of His great love for you!

Day 39

NAGGING THOUGHTS

Give all your worries and cares to God, for he cares about you.
1 PETER 5:7 NLT

You know the thing that happened this week that you can't seem to let go of? Those intrusive thoughts that seem to take up so much space in your mind? The cares and worries that you just can't seem to shake? God doesn't just want to hear about those things; He wants you to give them to Him—fully and completely. He wants you to live a life free of worries, anxieties, and fears so that you can live an abundant life that honors Him and fulfill the purposes He has for you.

Sounds pretty good, right? The problem is that some days it feels impossible to hand everything over to God and free yourself of the burdens you carry. Your worries and cares still weigh heavy on your mind. This is where another promise from God comes in. Philippians 4:6-7 says, "Do not be anxious about anything, but in every situation, by prayer and petition, with thanksgiving, present your requests to God. And the peace of God, which transcends all understanding, will guard your hearts and your minds in Christ Jesus." In every situation, we can bring our worries before God through prayer, and He will give us His peace.

Some days—when I'm stressing over an unhappy customer, worried about a deadline I am behind on meeting, trying to soothe my two-year-old and make sure my girls are getting their homework done, while figuring out how to have a somewhat nutritious dinner at a reasonable time—I forget to bring God into it all. I forget to pray and surrender every moment to Him. That doesn't mean that God is going to cook dinner or help my daughters with their homework (though I'm sure He'd be much better at it), but it means that I would be inviting Him to walk alongside me through it all and He would equip me with the peace I need to sustain me.

PRAYER: I want to bring this moment before You, God. My to-do list is long, and my worries are piling up. Help me to bring every worry to You today and come to You in every situation. Thank You for caring for me and extending Your peace to me.

DO THE HARD THING: Set a reminder for five different times throughout the day. Set aside two minutes each time to bring all your worries to God.

Day 40

REPLACING JEALOUSY WITH JOY

So may we never be arrogant, or look down on another, for each of us is an original. We must forsake all jealousy that diminishes the value of others. GALATIANS 5:26 TPT

Have you ever felt green with envy? I don't like to admit it, but I sure have: *Why does her life seem so perfect? Why does her husband make her breakfast in bed? Why does everything she touch turn to gold? I wish I could go on a vacation like that, have a home like that, or drive a car like that. Why did she get chosen for that promotion? Why is she always asked to speak or highlighted in our company? I wish I did presentations as well as her; it isn't fair.* I feel so childish writing out these thoughts, but even at almost forty years old, I have wrestled with these feelings.

How do we overcome envy and jealousy? First, we need to acknowledge we're battling those feelings. Healing begins when we acknowledge and confess our struggles to the Lord. Next, we need to avoid comparison. Do not fall victim to the comparison trap. Recognize that you have been uniquely designed just as you are. The Lord gave you specific gifts and talents and you have a special calling on your life. You're called to be you and no one else. And last, lean on the Lord with prayer. When thoughts of jealousy come, my immediate prayer is Psalm 51:10: "Create in me a pure heart, O God, and renew a steadfast spirit within me."

I want to be the kind of woman who cheers on those around me. I do not want to have to unfollow someone on social media because I'm jealous. I want to be the type of person who can not only like and comment on their photos but also be genuinely happy for them. The Lord can transform our hearts when we ask Him to. We do not have to try to have a change of heart alone. We serve a God who can replace our jealousy with joy.

PRAYER: God, I pray that You would replace any jealousy in my heart with joy. I pray that I would be able to support and celebrate those around me who are experiencing success.

DO THE HARD THING: Have you been dealing with jealousy? Look at what Scripture says. Read Romans 12:3-8; 2 Corinthians 10:12; Galatians 1:10; Philippians 2:3; and 1 Corinthians 12:1-31. On a note card, write out one Scripture from these passages that resonated with you; keep this verse with you at all times. Whenever you feel like you're about to compare yourself to someone else, read your verse and commit your gifts to God.

Day 41

RESTLESS WORLD

Peace I leave with you; my peace I give you. I do not give to you as the world gives. Do not let your hearts be troubled and do not be afraid. JOHN 14:27

The world seems to move a million miles a minute, and I feel like I can't keep up with the news, trends, or evolving technology. By the time I get through one anxiety-inducing headline, there are ten more equally devastating ones. It leaves me feeling quite hopeless at times.

But God does not give to us as the world does. The world gives us trouble, restlessness, and discontent; God gives us peace and fills us with hope. He and His Word are unchanging. While everything in the world flips and changes, God never does; He is our rock, our solid ground. The world is withholding, but God loves to give His children good gifts (see Matthew 7:11).

I think sometimes we believe the lie that God changes based on circumstance. We see the way the world is changing and the current events evolving in society. However, in the midst of all the change, we serve a God who is the same yesterday today and forever! He is not worried about what is changing. He does not get pushed around like a boat in the middle of a storm. He is constant, consistent, and steady. When you are restless with the things of this world, find comfort in knowing that with the Lord directing your life, there is hope and comfort!

PRAYER: Lord, sometimes I look at the world around me and only see trouble. I praise You for never changing and for being the solid ground I can stand on. Please replace my fear with Your peace and hope, even as I encounter the troubles of the world around me. I pray that I would be a light in the darkness.

DO THE HARD THING: Jot down a few things that are troubling you. In a different color of ink, write over the list "God's Peace > My Fears."

Day 42

TAKING THOUGHTS CAPTIVE

We take captive every thought to make it obedient to Christ.
2 CORINTHIANS 10:5

What was the first thought you had when you looked in the mirror this morning? I hope it was, "Hey, hot stuff, you really just woke up like this, huh?" But if you're like me, it was probably something more akin to, "Oof, we've gotta do something about these bags."

When we let insecurity and negative thoughts about ourselves run free in our minds, it takes a toll on us and steals our joy. God doesn't just want to give us a tolerable or decent life; He wants to give us life to the fullest! And to embrace that life, we need to fully replace our own self-image with how God sees us. When we live a life aligned with our identity in God, we experience unadulterated, full life.

Replacing our identity with the one God has for us isn't an easy process though. As women we've been trained to fixate on our insecurities. We tend to view negative thoughts about ourselves as "humble," when they're actually detrimental to our growth. But Scripture tells us to "take every thought captive" (2 Corinthians 10:5 NLT). That means that when you wake up in the morning and start zooming in on all the flaws, you need to take a moment, step back, and decide that you won't let that thought have control over you or your day. You take the power back from your thoughts and fill your mind with your God-given identities instead.

You're a masterpiece. You're a child of God, a daughter of the King. You're fearfully and wonderfully made. Your body is a temple of the Holy Spirit. You have a purpose and a future. You're forgiven. You're loved. You're beautiful.

PRAYER: God, I confess that I don't always have the nicest things to say about myself. I pray that today You would help me take those negative thoughts captive and replace them with truths and identities that You've spoken over me.

DO THE HARD THING: Take one of the identities written above and write it on your mirror or on a sticky note you'll see throughout the day. Try to wear that identity today, and when negative thoughts come your way, take them captive and replace them with the truth.

Day 43

HAIR COUNT

And the very hairs on your head are all numbered.
LUKE 12:7A NLT

I used to wonder if God kept track of all our hair counts. If I lost a hair in the shower, I imagined there being a tracker in heaven and the number decreasing by one. I know that's silly and not how it works. (Who's to say for sure?) But all those imaginings are beside the point. This verse is less about hair and more about the personal and intimate nature of our relationship with God. It also highlights His sovereignty and limitlessness.

There are almost eight billion people in the world, and God knows each one. No one was created by chance or accident. God has a plan for all of us, and He knows us intimately, even down to the number of hairs on our heads. This is displayed countless times in the Bible, including in the story of the woman at the well. Jesus went to get water from a well, and He found a woman there who was an outcast in her community. Not only did Jesus know everything about her, but He also took time to sit down and talk with her, extend grace and salvation, and answer her questions. This is the same care God has for us.

I don't know about you, but sometimes I think, *God doesn't care about my silly little problems. I'll just bring Him the big stuff and take care of the small stuff on my own.* This is probably the Enemy whispering in my ear because it is a straight-up lie. If God cares about the hairs on your head and knitted you together in your mother's womb, then He cares about the bully in your daughter's third-grade class and the things at work that you're really proud of. God sees it all and He wants us to invite Him into it all.

PRAYER: God, thank You for desiring to have a relationship with me and for caring about all the details of my life. Help me to remember to invite You into both the big and small moments of my day.

DO THE HARD THING: Try to count the hairs on your head—just kidding! Try to bring even your smallest worries, inconveniences, and thoughts before God today. He wants you to share it all!

Day 44

HOLD MY BAGGAGE

Therefore, since we are surrounded by such a great cloud of witnesses, let us throw off every encumbrance and the sin that so easily entangles, and let us run with endurance the race set out for us. Let us fix our eyes on Jesus, the author and perfecter of our faith, who for the joy set before Him endured the cross, scorning its shame, and sat down at the right hand of the throne of God. **HEBREWS 12:1-2 BSB**

I'm an over-packer. This is something I've accepted about myself, and I don't see any point in changing. In my opinion, it's always better to be overprepared than underprepared, so yes, I have three different outfits for any given day: what if I go swimming and then get a last-minute invite to a black-tie wedding on the same day? But let me tell you, being an over-packer and being late to the airport aren't a good combination. Rolling a giant checked bag, carrying the largest carry-on bag allowed, and holding a giant purse weighs a sister down. It's pretty hard to rush to Gate 12 with all that baggage.

I think we hold onto emotional and spiritual baggage that weighs us down in our walk with God. Whether it's a sin we're struggling to break free from, a broken friendship that still causes deep pain when we think about it, or unforgiveness in our hearts—whatever weighs on us—God wants us to release that baggage. He wants us to throw off everything that burdens and entangles us so we can run the race He has for us without any hindrances.

God has a purpose and plan for each one of us. When we're weighed down by sin and intrusive thoughts, we take our eyes off Jesus and the path He has for us, and we set our eyes on earthly things that won't last and will leave us unsatisfied. Throw off what is weighing you down and fix your eyes on Jesus.

PRAYER: God, it feels like I'm carrying a lot of baggage right now. I want to fix my eyes on You, but I keep getting distracted by things of this world. Help me to throw off everything that burdens me and the sins that entangle me so I can focus on You and the path You've set before me.

DO THE HARD THING: Picture a suitcase full of your struggles, worries, and sins—everything that weighs heavy on your heart and mind. Now picture yourself handing over the suitcase full of worries to God. Try to live today baggage free.

Day 45

CHOOSING KINDNESS

Since God chose you to be the holy people he loves, you must clothe yourselves with tenderhearted mercy, kindness, humility, gentleness, and patience. COLOSSIANS 3:12 NLT

Have you ever had to deal with mean people? (Cue the Taylor Swift song "Mean.") Maybe it is the mean mom clique at your kid's school; they act nice to your face and then you hear about them talking behind your back. Or maybe it is just some troll from the internet who takes the time to make a fake profile to leave you hurtful, cruel comments. Or maybe it is the flat-out rude sales associate who obviously hates her job and feels the need to take it out on you. Some of you may even have to deal with mean family members. It can be hard not to dish right back what we're served, but God calls us higher.

The truth is that we can't let mean people, hurtful words, unkind actions, or negative opinions of others ruin our day, hold us back, or dim our light. God calls us to be light in the darkness and to be in the world but not of the world. I know my battle isn't against flesh and blood but "against the spiritual forces of evil in the heavenly realms" (Ephesians 6:12). What the devil may try to use for bad, God can turn around and use for good.

Jesus Christ Himself was treated horribly by mean people while He walked this earth, and yet He said, "Father, forgive them, for they do not know what they are doing" (Luke 23:34). So as hard as it is, I'll try to do what Matthew 5:44 says: love my enemies and pray for those who persecute me. Hurting people hurt people. Where there is meanness, there is also deep pain. The most effective response to meanness is compassion. No matter how I feel, I will choose kindness. After all, someday I'll be living in a big old city on a hill.

PRAYER: Lord, help me choose kindness today and extend compassion to everyone. Help me see the hurting people around me and be Your hands and feet on this earth.

DO THE HARD THING: List the names of a few people who have been mean to you who you need to pray for and forgive. Now search your heart. Who have you treated poorly who you might need to ask for forgiveness?

Day 46

TRUST

Let the morning bring me word of your unfailing love, for I have put my trust in you. Show me the way I should go, for to you I entrust my life. **PSALM 143:8**

Trust—a small word but incredibly hard to live out. I will admit I'm an obsessive, type-A, control freak. I prefer to be in charge; I like knowing the ball is my court and I want to handle it all. When I want something, I typically want it now. I want to speed up the process, and if I'm completely honest, I want things to go according to my schedule and my timeline.

The problem is that I see things from a mere human perspective and God sees things from an eternal perspective; He has the bird's-eye view of life. I have learned that the Lord wants me to relinquish control and place my trust in Him. I don't know what is best, even though I may think I do. God's ways are perfect, His timing is perfect, and He knows what is best for me and the situation I so badly want to control. John 13:7 puts it perfectly: "You do not realize now what I am doing, but later you will understand."

PRAYER: Lord, give me the kind of trust Noah had when he built an ark during a drought. Give me patience during the waiting time, help me to surrender everything to You, and give me the ability to rely on You in both the wait and the pursuit.

DO THE HARD THING: Name something that isn't fitting your preferred timeline. Surrender it to God and trust that His timing for it is perfect.

Day 47

KNOW WHOSE YOU ARE

But you are a chosen people, a royal priesthood, a holy nation, God's special possession, that you may declare the praises of him who called you out of darkness into his wonderful light.
1 PETER 2:9

The older I get, the more roles I have: wife, mom, business owner, church member, volunteer, friend, and the list goes on. Those roles and responsibilities are beautiful and rewarding. I love them all—and I'm a firm believer in giving my all wherever I am and in whatever I'm doing. I'm an all or nothing girl. But in the past year, the Lord has had to teach me some valuable lessons regarding who I am.

It can be so easy to find fulfillment in the task, role, responsibility you're carrying; that's not necessarily a bad thing. I love being a wife to my husband, a mom to my three children, and running a business where I lead a team of thousands, but I can't find my identity solely in those roles.

When I become consumed with my job and overly focused on the recognitions, the next promotion, or working harder and harder, I quickly start to place my identity in that job. I feel only as good as my performance, so when nobody notices my hard work, I start to feel insecure. Even when I reach the promotion or get the award, it feels great for a moment, but then I'm left feeling empty. Why? Because I forgot who I am; I forgot whose I am and what my true identity is.

Your value isn't found in how much you work, your achievements or status, what you do for your kids, how many likes you get on social media, what home or clothes you have, or what event or party you have or haven't been invited to. We can't place our value in anything other than Christ and being children of the King. The applause will fade, the children will grow up, your spouse will fail you at some point. But when you look to the One who will never leave you nor forsake you and will always love you regardless of what you do, then and only then will you be completely fulfilled.

PRAYER: As I tackle all my responsibilities today, help me remember my true identity. Before I'm anything else, I'm Your child. Only when I find my identity in You am I fulfilled.

DO THE HARD THING: What roles or things might you be placing your identity in other than being a child of the King?

Day 48

TRUE HAPPINESS

Make me walk along the path of your commands, for that is where my happiness is found. PSALM 119:35 NLT

When I think of happiness, I think of my kids on Christmas morning—right when they wake up, before we open any presents. Or on the last day of school when they rush inside to put their swimsuits on for their first swim of the summer. It's true and utter bliss.

When we grow older, the happiness of our childhood days seems to grow a little dimmer; we tend to leave it behind with other childhood things. But happiness isn't reserved for kids on Christmas morning. True happiness, joy, is a result of walking in accordance with God's Word. God has gifts, blessings, and promises in store for us each day. When we expectantly and joyfully wait on God for those gifts, blessings, and promises, we're like kids on Christmas morning—and that is where happiness is found.

I'm not saying life will be a walk in the park; when we walk with God, we still face challenges, struggles, and pain. But when we're in step with God, challenges aren't just challenges; they're challenges with purpose. Struggles are clothed in glory. Pain is lined with hope. That purpose, glory, and hope is something to be happy about.

PRAYER: Lord, I want to walk in step with You today. Please open my eyes to the gifts, blessings, and promises along the path You have for me. Fill me with the true happiness that only comes from walking through life with You.

DO THE HARD THING: It's easy to find happiness when everything is going right. But as problems and inconveniences come up, try to find the happiness that God has promised you. Maybe even keep a small notebook with you where you can write out all the happy moments, too.

Day 49

PUT THE MEASURING TAPE AWAY

Therefore encourage one another and build each other up, just as in fact you are doing. **1 THESSALONIANS 5:11**

Comparison and jealousy have a way of making us pit ourselves against other people as if life were a competition. When I see someone else's business doing well, I think about my own and wonder if it measures up—if I measure up. When we let comparison turn opportunities for connection into competition, we miss out on some of the fullness of life.

When we compare ourselves to other women, we train ourselves to tear one another down and pick one another apart. It can be daunting for me to see what someone else is doing and feel like I could never achieve that. But the thing is, I'm not supposed to achieve that! When we get caught up in comparing ourselves to someone else, we lose sight of what we're destined to do. You're enough for what you're destined for. When we live from our enoughness, we're quicker to celebrate people around us.

We're called to encourage and build one another up. We can't do that when we have our measuring tape out! Put the measuring tape away and stop comparing someone else's dream and destiny to your own. The world is big enough for all our dreams. When we choose connection and encouragement rather than comparison and competition, we're choosing to live life to its fullest measure.

PRAYER: Lord, thank You for calling me and giving me a purpose and a dream. I pray that as I look to those around me who are following their dreams, I would push past any temptations to compare and be quick to offer encouragement and support. Help me build up others.

DO THE HARD THING: In what area of your life are you most likely to fall into the comparison trap? Today, when you find yourself pulling out the measuring tape to measure your success against someone else's, stop yourself and choose to encourage the other person instead.

Day 50

THE BEST PATHWAY

The LORD says, "I will guide you along the best pathway for your life. I will advise and watch over you."
PSALM 32:8 NLT

Do you ever find yourself standing in an aisle of the grocery store for five full minutes because you can't decide between three nearly identical pasta sauces? Sometimes even the small decisions are hard. The sheer volume of decisions we make day to day can be overwhelming. It's important to remember that we're never alone in our decision-making though. God, an expert of our lives, and all things really, is right alongside us, and He knows the best pathway for our lives.

Waiting on God and asking for His guidance can be frustrating. This reminds me of a story about Gideon in the Bible. Gideon sought guidance from God about whether God would rescue His people during battle. Gideon said, "If you are truly going to use me to rescue Israel as you promised, prove it to me in this way. I will put a wool fleece on the threshing floor tonight. If the fleece is wet with dew in the morning but the ground is dry, then I will know that you are going to help me rescue Israel as you promised" (Judges 6:36-37 NLT). And God did as Gideon requested. But that wasn't enough for Gideon. He followed up the next day and said to God, "'Please don't be angry with me, but let me make one more request. Let me use the fleece for one more test. This time let the fleece remain dry while the ground around it is wet with dew.' So that night God did as Gideon asked. The fleece was dry in the morning, but the ground was covered with dew" (Judges 6:39-40 NLT).

When we seek guidance from God, Gideon's fleece test doesn't always work. (Believe me, I've tried.) Most of the time, the ways God guides us are more subtle, but when we're in close communication with Him, we can better discern His voice and where He is leading us. So, draw near to the Lord, seek His face, go to Him with every concern or decision you need to make, and He will be faithful to guide you. Who knows? Maybe He'll send a wet fleece our way.

PRAYER: Thank You for Your goodness and love. Thank You for watching over me and guiding me. Please let me hear Your voice today, God, and help me know what Your path for me is. Amen.

DO THE HARD THING: Talk to God about all your decisions today, big and small, and see if you can hear His voice guiding you.

Day 51

OVERCOMING FAILURE

I can do all things through Christ who gives me strength.
PHILIPPIANS 4:13 BSB

Do you remember failing your first test in school? If you have never failed a test, just imagine the time you first made a B or, for the rarest bunch, the lowest A. Immediately upon turning over the paper and looking at that number written and circled at the top, your stomach dropped. Failure stings. Even when we're past our testing days, we still get that same stomach-dropping feeling when we don't get the job we applied for or when we lose our temper with our kids—again.

It's not falling, being rejected, or making a mistake that matters; it is what you decide to do after that counts. Sometimes it takes being told no to ignite the fire that propels you to move forward and fight for that yes! We must shift our perspective from thinking of any failure, rejection, or mistake as a step backward and reorient ourselves to think of failures as still moving us toward our dreams. If you look for it, after that first sting of failure passes, you can see that you got a little closer to your dream, learned something about yourself, and became stronger through the process. You can fail forward. Failure doesn't have to end with the sting if you decide not to let go of your dream.

Philippians 4:13 is God's great encouragement to us when we start feeling overcome by failure: "I can do all things through Christ who gives me strength" (BSB). This should be our response every time doubts, excuses, and fears of failure swarm in our minds. Any time you think, *I can't—I can't go back to school,* or *I can't make it as an artist,* or *I can't run a marathon*—replace it with *I can through Christ who gives me strength.* We can't do it on our own, but anything is possible with God (see Matthew 19:26). So dream big and don't let failure hold you back. A no always means God has a bigger yes in store.

PRAYER: God, thank You for Your goodness and strength. Thank You for placing dreams in my heart. I pray for the courage and strength to pursue my dreams even in the face of failure. While falling and failing always sting, I know You're always there to pick me up again.

DO THE HARD THING: Are there any dreams you've let go of because of failure? What if you decided that the road didn't end there? Find a way to move forward with that dream today. How can you fail forward?

Day 52

VISION

Where there is no vision, the people perish.
PROVERBS 29:18 KJV

Have you ever gone on a walk in a new city and each time you reached a crossroad, you picked whichever direction felt right? Then, thirty minutes and ten Taylor Swift songs later, you look up and have absolutely no idea where you are? Thank God for technology; without it, I'd still be wandering around somewhere in San Diego. Going through seasons of our lives without vision is like mindlessly walking around in a new city—you'll end up lost, a little confused, and way off track.

Vision fuels and connects us; it's what allows us to grow even in dry seasons. We all have dreams; we need vision to bring those dreams into reality. Vision is the only way to accomplish world-changing things. Creating a vision of yourself truly living your dream only leads to growth and prosperity.

You may not think about yourself as a visionary or dreamer, but you don't have to identify as a visionary to cultivate vision. It's something you can grow in, like a muscle you must work out daily. Picture where you want to be and what you want to achieve and let your vision fuel you throughout your day. With vision and trust in God's plan for you, every step you take leads you toward your dream.

PRAYER: God, give me Your vision for the season You have me in. There are dreams I believe You placed in my heart—please help me have the vision to practically bring my dreams to life.

DO THE HARD THING: Think about the dreams God has placed in your heart. Maybe think of that one big dream that makes your heart beat a little faster. Imagine yourself accomplishing that dream and then start cultivating vision for how to achieve it.

Day 53

THE THING ABOUT SETBACKS

But as for you, be strong and do not give up, for your work will be rewarded. 2 CHRONICLES 15:7

Have you ever felt like for every step you take forward, you take two steps backward? It's easy to feel like you're failing or falling short when you're building something, working toward a goal, or trying to fix a situation. During these moments, quitting can seem like the easiest answer. But is it really? When I think about times I almost quit, I'm so glad I persevered. I know it would be so much harder to look back in regret at what I walked away from than it is to keep going when it feels tough.

Those times we want to quit are the perfect times to press into Jesus, our Source of strength! In our weak and weary moments, His power and strength will be evident in and through us.

In 1 Samuel 16, David, a shepherd boy, was anointed to be king. But that prophecy wouldn't be fulfilled for many years. King Saul, who knew of this prophecy, wanted David killed. David had to run, hide in caves, and survive on whatever food his few loyal men could find. What would have happened if David had quit when Saul was trying to kill him? David could have said, "Never mind, I'm going off the grid—forget this future king business!" But he didn't. He trusted the Lord and His plan and His perfect timing.

It's not always easy to stay the course, especially when you get knocked down. Often times our setbacks become our greatest setups. So don't give up. The world needs what you've got! Your dream is worth it, you're worth it, and the lives you'll impact are worth it. I'm sure you have heard it said that the greater the battle is, the greater the victory will be. Keep your eyes fixed on the prize ahead.

PRAYER: I want to quit today, God. Please give me the strength I need to make it through the day. I trust that You are working everything together for good; please increase my faith!

DO THE HARD THING: What are some goals or dreams you're currently working toward? What are some setbacks you've faced? Ask God to turn those into setups for success!

Day 54

EQUIPPED FOR WHAT-IFS

For God has not given us a spirit of fear, but of power and of love and of a sound mind. 2 TIMOTHY 1:7 NKJV

Have you ever felt an overwhelming, even suffocating fear? Maybe it's fear of failure, fear of being hurt, fear of the unknown, fear of what could happen. Fear will hold you back; it can paralyze you and ultimately keep you from living your life to the fullest.

One day, I was allowing fear to creep in. As I began to pray, the Lord reminded me to let my faith be greater than my fear. I can let my mind run wild with all of the what-ifs, or I can say, "Lord, I put my faith and trust in You. The One who has promised that though I walk through the valley of the shadow of death I shall fear no evil because You're with me" (Psalm 23:4, author's paraphrase).

Raising kids during a pandemic—honestly even just living through a pandemic—can feel so incredibly scary. I have dealt with all the fears, like so many others during this time. But time and time again, I remind myself to hand over my fear and trust my heavenly Father who is in complete control. It's not easy to surrender everything to Him, especially when the world feels so out of control and every time I flip through the TV channels my worries multiply. But this entire pandemic is no surprise to God; He saw this from the beginning, and He knows how it will end.

He has equipped you and your family with power, love, and a sound mind for such a time as this (see 2 Timothy 1:7). There are no mistakes with Him. So cast your cares on Him. Replace your fear with faith and let the Prince of Peace comfort you, guide you, and help you navigate the unknowns. Stop focusing on the storm and fix your eyes on the One who can calm any storm. You're not alone, my friend.

PRAYER: Lord, thank You that You're sovereign in every season. I pray that when my heart fills with fear, Your peace would wash over me. Thank You for equipping me with Your power and love. Help me rely on You through all the unknowns the day brings.

DO THE HARD THING: What fears, worries, or cares might you need to surrender to the Lord today?

Day 55

TRADING TRAGEDY FOR TESTIMONY

If anyone is in Christ, he is a new creation; the old has passed away, and see, the new has come!
2 CORINTHIANS 5:17 CSB

There are two key ideas I've taken hold of to move on from my past: release and embrace. When we release ourselves from the past, we no longer remain bound by the pain, guilt, or shame. This doesn't mean you forget everything about the past; it just means you don't let it have control over you, your thoughts, or your emotions. This is where the second idea comes in: embrace. Embrace the lessons learned, let go, and keep moving forward.

I was a competitive gymnast as a child, and let's just say the gym culture in the '90s was extremely different than today. (Thank goodness for progress!) I had weigh-ins and had to keep a food journal. There was a lot of pressure to be a certain size as a young gymnast, and it didn't take long for me to be overly concerned with my weight. I developed an eating disorder as a young teen. For years, I would binge eat and purge and abuse diet pills and laxatives. When I was eighteen years old, I was healed and set free from this awful eating disorder.

For years, I stayed quiet about my struggle because I was embarrassed; I just swept it under the rug. Over a decade later, I joined a health and wellness company. I loved the plant-based products, and I was excited about the business opportunity, but there was one problem—my past. Who was I to share about healthy living when I used to mistreat my body? I felt like a phony. Praise the Lord it didn't take long for me to realize that my past had no bearing on my future; I wasn't the same person. I had to release my past and let go of the shame. I then had to acknowledge that the Lord gave me a message through my mess. I now knew how to live a healthy life, and I had a testimony of God's healing power that I could share with other girls who struggled like I once did. I had lessons that I could now embrace as a part of my story.

When our identity is firmly rooted in God and His promises for us, we can more easily let go of the pain from our past and use the lessons learned from it to benefit others. If you've walked through hell and back, I bet you anything that someone needs your story. You overcame your past and became a new creation—that's a huge victory! It takes a warrior to trade tragedy for testimony. And being able to do that is part of embracing the new identity God has given you.

PRAYER: Lord, help me release my past and the parts of my identity that aren't of You, and help me embrace the lessons You're teaching me.

DO THE HARD THING: What is something from your past that you can release today, and what lesson can you embrace in its place? Ask God for an opportunity to share your story with someone.

Day 56

SEASONS

There is a time for everything, and a season for every activity under the heavens. ECCLESIASTES 3:1

Have you ever taken on too much in one season? The first year I started my business, it was hard. I worked a ton. I was a stay-at-home mom with two girls, served as the women's ministry director, and co-led the young adult ministry with my husband. That year was pure chaos. When my oldest daughter started preschool, I made the hasty decision to sign up to be the room mom. I made this choice not because I had oodles of time on my hands but because of my mom guilt. I felt bad for working, so I thought I needed to compensate for it by doing more. That year I forgot about the end-of-year pre-school party (total mom fail). I had a total breakdown in the school parking lot, with both my daughters wide-eyed and probably terrified in their car seats. I realized I was overcommitted and couldn't keep up. As a result, I didn't present a good version of myself to anyone or anything. That was the last time I spread myself that thin and the moment I learned it was okay to say no.

When we begin pursuing our dreams, we have to pay attention to our capacity and capabilities in each season. We must remember that every season is different. You may be capable of doing more in the spring because you have more time, your overall mood is better, you feel more energized, and the sun is out longer. You shouldn't force yourself to keep up with the same activities in the fall when your kids are going back to school and circumstances aren't the same. Evaluate what you need in each season and don't do things out of guilt or obligation. Protecting your time and your priorities is part of living out of abundance rather than scarcity.

There's a time for everything, which means there's a time to pursue that dream on your heart. Make time to say yes to things that will help you get closer to your dreams.

PRAYER: You're my number-one priority; everything I am and everything I have comes from You. Please help me protect my time and energy in this season and go wherever You lead me.

DO THE HARD THING: Evaluate the season you're in. Make a list of all your responsibilities. Take note of the energy and time you have. Are you working to pursue your dreams at all? What needs to change for you to be able to pursue a dream on your heart?

Day 57

TREASURE AND PONDER

Devote yourselves to prayer, being watchful and thankful.
COLOSSIANS 4:2

You know when you're locked in on a task and chaos could break loose around you but you'd have no idea because you're in the zone? Sometimes I think we get this way about ourselves too; we're so zoned in on what we need, our schedules, and our responsibilities that we forget to look at our surroundings, the glory in our circumstances, and the beauty in the chaos.

Devoting ourselves to prayer isn't just about asking God for things we want or need; it includes inviting Him into all our moments, big and small, and keeping our eyes open, looking for God's blessings everywhere we go and giving thanks to Him in all circumstances.

When I think of someone who was watchful and thankful, I think of Mary, the mother of Jesus. Everything seemingly went wrong on the day Jesus was born. First, Mary and Joseph were traveling. (Imagine being on a road trip on your due date!) Then they couldn't find any rooms available in inns. So they went to a nearby stable and placed Jesus in a feeding trough when He was born. Talk about un-ideal circumstances. But Luke 2:19 says, "But Mary treasured up all these things and pondered them in her heart."

Next time nothing is going according to plan, take a moment to treasure and ponder. You never know how God might be using those exact circumstances for His glory. We can truly find some good in most circumstances; the lens through which we look at the situation matters.

PRAYER: Lord, thank You so much for all You're doing in my life. Thank You for always being with me; I couldn't do any of this without You. Please help me look outside of myself today and be watchful and thankful for how You're working in the world around me.

DO THE HARD THING: As you go about your day, look around you and find five things that bring joy or peace to your heart. Express thanks to God for allowing you to notice the blessing in the moment.

Day 58

DON'T RUSH; BE STILL

Be still and know that I am God. I will be exalted among the nations, I will be exalted in the earth. PSALM 46:10

As you're reading this devotion, my bet is that you looked at how long it is and have already started thinking ahead toward the rest of the day. That's my bet because that's exactly what I would do (and exactly what I did while writing it).

You've probably heard the story of Mary and Martha, but as a refresher: Mary and Martha were friends of Jesus. Once when Jesus was at their home, Martha was busy preparing everything and trying to be a good hostess while Mary was sitting at Jesus' feet and listening to Him. Martha got mad that Mary wasn't helping her, and Jesus rebuked Martha, telling her, "Mary has chosen what is better" (Luke 10:42).

Now you go-getters who like getting things done—those of you who frequently carried the team on group projects—are probably rolling your eyes right now. But don't miss what's at play here. Jesus didn't say there was never a time or place for preparation, cleaning, cooking, fulfilling duties and responsibilities—of course there is! But Jesus wants us to be still before Him and know He is God before we even lift a hand to work—to humble ourselves before Him and know everything in our lives, everything we accomplish, comes from Him and is for Him and making His name known. Martha wasn't wrong; she just got ahead of herself.

I can remember a specific season in my life when I was so consumed and busy doing ministry—the outreaches, children's church, women's ministry, and small groups—that I forgot to pause and spend time with the Lord. I was more consumed with my church to-do list than being in communion with the One who matters. Start today by being still in God's presence.

PRAYER: Thank You for loving me and giving me the gift of Your constant presence through the Holy Spirit. You're powerful and mighty and sovereign. You hold everything in Your hands, You know the future, and You know the plans You have for me. Help me be still before You in Your power today.

DO THE HARD THING: Are you getting ahead of yourself like Martha, or are you posturing your heart like Mary? Lay everything that needs to get done to the side for a minute and sit at Jesus's feet.

Day 59

COMFORT ZONE

Who knows if perhaps you were made queen for just such a time as this? ESTHER 4:14 NLT

I like to feel comfortable, and I like familiarity. Change can be hard for me because I'm a creature of habit. When I started my business seven years ago, I took a huge step outside my comfort zone. I wish I could say it was an easy decision, but it wasn't! I had to go through all the emotions and thoughts of beginning something new! *Would I fail? Would it be hard? What if I didn't have what it took?* If we're not careful, our fearful thoughts can keep us from everything God has in store for us.

I had a choice: I could stay where I was, stuck in my fearful thoughts about starting my own business, or I could listen to the gentle nudge of the Holy Spirit to step out in faith. It was not easy, but I can promise you, great things seldom happen in your comfort zone. I've experienced the most victories and growth in life when I get a little bit—maybe even extremely—uncomfortable.

When I think of someone in the Bible getting uncomfortable, I think of Esther. She went before the king to save her people even though it could have meant her death. As she was trying to decide whether to go before the king, her fearful thoughts almost got the better of her. But then her uncle challenged her and said, "Perhaps you were made queen for just such a time as this." Because of her step forward, she changed the world and saved many lives.

I'm here to tell you, like Uncle Mordecai told Esther, "Perhaps you were made for such a time as this." Don't let fear, comfort, or excuses get in the way of fulfilling your purpose and dream. Take the first step!

PRAYER: Lord, please give me courage and faith like Esther today. Help me step out of my comfort zone to further glorify You with my life.

DO THE HARD THING: What is one step you can take toward your purpose or dream today?

Day 60

WHAT'S IN YOUR HAND?

His divine power has given us everything we need for a godly life through our knowledge of him who called us by his own glory and goodness. 2 PETER 1:3

I don't have anything to offer. Everyone around me is so gifted and talented. I wish I could be a gifted speak like her. I wish I had the influence she has. Why wasn't I born into a family like that? It would be so much easier if I had those types of resources and connections. I feel like the underdog.

Have you ever thought like that? Many times in my life, I was too busy noticing other people's gifts to look at what the Lord had placed in my hand for such a time as this. What the Lord has given you is more than enough. We have to be on guard so that we don't fall into the traps of comparison, envy, jealousy, or feelings of unworthiness.

Living a life of enoughness, I believe, is right in line with the heart of Jesus. When I think of people who feel like they aren't enough or don't have much to offer, I think of the widow who gave her last two mites. If you read the story in Mark 12:41-44, you can see that Jesus was more pleased with the poor widow's two small coins than with the rich who put tons of money into the treasury. Although it seemed like the rich gave the most, the widow actually gave more. The wealthy gave out of what they could very well spare, but the widow gave her livelihood, despite her poverty. She gave enough.

I also think of the boy who offered up his five loaves of bread and two fish to feed five thousand. The boy saw a huge need, met it by giving what he had, and it was blessed by God! It didn't matter that his offering looked meager. He still gave it all. He held nothing back. I can't help but think of what his mom might have felt; she likely never thought the silent work of her hands in her kitchen would feed a multitude for Jesus. You never ever know what God has planned with even the most seemingly insignificant somethings we have to give.

Mary, the mother of Jesus, comes to mind too. She was young, probably someone easily overlooked in her village, but she had a willing spirit. When the angel of the Lord came to her and told her she would carry the Messiah, she trusted God.

That small coin, that lunch of bread and fish, and that willing spirit may have seemed unimportant and even insignificant at the time, but centuries later, we're still learning lessons from these great people of faith. The widow, the boy, and Mary all stepped out in faith and used what they had in their hand to change their world.

You have a sphere of influence right now that you can reach with what you have. Don't miss out on the opportunities and divine appointments right in front of you because you think you have nothing to offer or are too busy comparing yourself to others. The world needs you to show up as yourself with what you have in your hands right now. Who knows who will read and learn lessons from your story centuries from now? How completely freeing it is to live a life knowing you're enough just as you are.

PRAYER: Lord, help me to acknowledge the special, unique, one-of-a-kind gifts You have given me. Help me to open my eyes and be aware of the people You have put in my path to influence for You. Help me to stop hiding, stop thinking I don't have anything to offer, and stop trying to be like someone else. I pray that today I decide to be the best version of me.

YOU CAN DO HARD THINGS: What are some of the gifts and opportunities the Lord has placed in your hand right now for this time?

ENDNOTES

1 Trevor Wheelwright TV, "Cell Phone Behavior Survey: Are People Addicted to Their Phones?" reviews.org, April 21, 2021, https://www.reviews.org/mobile/cell-phone-addiction/.

2 Robert L. Leahy, *The Worry Cure: Seven Steps to Stop Worry from Stopping You* (New York, NY: Three Rivers, 2005), 109.

3 Billy Graham, "When we come to the end of ourselves, we come to the beginning of God." Facebook, March 19, 2015, https://www.facebook.com/BillyGrahamEvangelisticAssociation/posts/when-we-come-to-the-end-of-ourselves-we-come-to-the-beginning-of-god-billy-graha/10155276694630328/.

4 "H7503 - rāp â – Strong's Hebrew Lexicon (KJV)," Blue Letter Bible, accessed August 31, 2021, https://www.blueletterbible.org/lexicon/h7503/kjv/wlc/0-1/.

SheriLynn Alcala is a wife, mom of three, entrepreneur, and the author of *You Can Do Hard Things: How to Ditch the Excuses & Achieve Your Dreams*. She is passionate about empowering other women to rise up, walk in their gifts, and pursue their dreams. SheriLynn lives in Dallas, Texas, with her family of five.

To purchase SheriLynn's first book, *You Can Do Hard Things,* visit www.youcanthebook.com

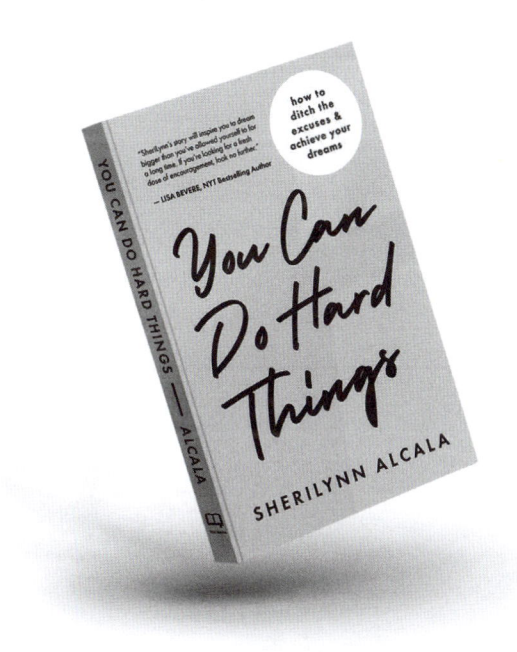

"SheriLynn's story will inspire you to dream bigger than you've allowed yourself to for a long time. If you're looking for a fresh dose of encouragement, look no further."

- LISA BEVERE
New York Times Best Selling Author